S

g
d
d

Joel Ha
&
Neil Ric

MITCHELL
BEAZLEY

CONTENTS

ONE

In Fine Spirits
AN INTRODUCTION

A very warm welcome to you, fellow spirits enthusiasts and curious quaffers, as well as to those entering the world of spirits for the first time.

»

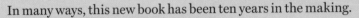

In many ways, this new book has been ten years in the making.

A decade ago, when our debut book, *Distilled*, was first published (now printed in multiple languages) an incredible landscape was emerging in the world of craft spirits – as was an entirely new kind of producer. For the first time, smaller spirits brands were being treated as equals to the long-established big names, both behind the bar and on the shelves of retailers the world over. The keenest minds in the drinks industry were thirsty for unusual, small batch and often obscure bottles which pushed the envelope of genres and traditional spirits categories, and challenged perceptions of flavour.

The same enthusiasm began to seep into the minds of you, the consumer. You began to seek out new, independent craft operations, searching not only for a more diverse flavour profile but for the fascinating stories behind the spirit in the bottle. What motivated these makers to push the boundaries of traditional production techniques? What inspired them to define the foundations of a new global craft spirits movement?

We were smitten too and *Distilled* was our way to pay homage to the craft spirits producers who we respected the most. From absinthe to whisky and everything in between, we tried to seek out the unusual, the uncanny and the incomparable. From spending time in Gascony with an artisanal Armagnac maker, who cooked us dinner in the fire of the portable still he tows behind his tractor, to the now legendary mezcal producer, who regaled us with hair-raising stories of smuggling drums of illegal booze over the Mexican border into the USA, *Distilled* marked a poignant awakening for us and changed our lives as both drinks writers and spirits enthusiasts.

Ten years later, we're as enthusiastic as ever. However, the global scene has expanded beyond all comprehension and today's drinker is far more knowledgeable and discerning with the things they enjoy drinking.

In Fine Spirits is, in many ways, the sequel to *Distilled*. Our appreciation of all things craft remains undimmed but this time we also wanted to express our fondness for the bigger, more well-known historical brands. We've looked at the process of making spirits around the world in more detail, and included a simple yet effective way to appraise the range of unique and highly diverse flavours. There's also a collection of interviews with spirits makers of every style, getting under the skin of what makes them tick.

So settle back, put a record on and pour yourself something classy, as you join us in discovering the finest spirits in the world.

Cheers, Joel & Neil

HOW
THIS BOOK
WORKS

Over the following pages you'll find a comprehensive global view of different spirits separated into their umbrella categories. Brandy (including a dedicated section on those from France, such as Cognac, Armagnac and Calvados) rum, gin, whisky from all over the world and agave-based spirits are given a brief introduction which explains the fundamentals of each spirit. We then explore their history, culture, production styles, offer up our favourite cocktail to try for each one and, in the 'Meet the Maker' sections, introduce you to some of the most important producers and founders in the world. Finally, we've curated a list of 'Ten to Try' in every category, which shines a light on a few highly unusual spirits, as well as some true classics. In each one, you'll also find a 'Best in Glass': a spirit which we deem to be at the pinnacle of excellence in every way and an essential brand to seek out for your collection.

But first! A section on deciphering flavours and aromas, so you can get the most from sampling spirits. We've tried to make the experience as universal as possible by creating a Flavour Descriptor framework. Each spirit category can be measured almost equally against each other by using 14 distinct building blocks to represent the suggested flavours and aromas you're likely to find.

TASTING NOTES

Discovering the Flavours & Aromas in Spirits

Given the incredibly diverse nature of global spirits, the raw materials from which they are distilled and the art of maturation – which in many cases, brings additional complexity and richness to the spirit – our noses and palates are confronted with an almighty challenge when identifying flavour and aroma. Even the world's greatest experts in spirits assessment face a similar dilemma when creating a lexicon to describe what's in the glass in front of them.

Any scientists reading this will be familiar with the chemical compounds which make up flavour and aroma: a complex combination of esters, alcohols, fatty acids, carbonyls, sulphur compounds, terpenoids, volatile phenols and heterocyclic compounds. However, this formidable-yet-essential group doesn't exactly trip off the tongue in everyday conversation with a friend or local bartender. Some simplification is most definitely needed.

Each spirit category has its own unique 'signature notes' which usually demonstrate to the drinker its origin, key raw materials and, in some cases, the type of wood it has been matured in. Spread this across more than a dozen different categories, however, and the outcome would lead to endless descriptive possibilities. Some tasters like to use colours to help describe what they're tasting (a process called synaesthesia). This might not apply to everyone but we find it helps to give a sense of direction to certain groups of flavours and aromas.

When it comes to the spirits in this book, we have tried to establish some key building blocks of both flavour and aroma which can be applied universally: a sort of spirits architectural plan if you like, helping you to decipher, decode – and ultimately categorize – what you're drinking into 14 distinct groups.

Of course, this list is not exhaustive, and indeed some spirits may fit into multiple categories. Besides which, the art of nosing and tasting spirits is a massively subjective and personal experience. Still, the following groups will hopefully broaden your own tasting note vocabulary and help the creative process when you're trying to describe the tantalizing host of aromas and flavours in your glass.

TURN TO INDIVIDUAL CHAPTERS FOR EACH SPIRIT'S PRINCIPAL FLAVOUR GROUPS.

GREEN FRUIT

Freshly sliced apples, white wine, ripe pears, gooseberries, kiwi

RED FRUIT

Raspberries, strawberries, blueberries, plums, jam

HERBAL

Fresh mint, thyme, rosemary, cut grass, pine needles

SPICY

Cinnamon, cloves, dried figs, pepper, ginger

CITRUS

Lemon zest, limes, orange juice, grapefruit

VEGETAL

Cooked carrots, tomato leaves, compost, root vegetables

CEREAL

Malt extract, porridge oats, sweetcorn, straw, fresh bread

WOODY

Polished furniture, freshly sawn oak, forest aromas, dried leaves

MINERAL

Salt, warm sand, chalk, stone floors, seashells

SMOKY

Toast, medicinal aromas, barbecued meat, log fires

FATTY

Butter, candle wax, suntan lotion, olive oil, fresh cream

FLORAL

Perfume, freshly cut and dried flowers, rosé wine, elderflower, lavender

NUTTY

Chopped walnuts, almonds, sherry, fresh leather, coffee, dark chocolate, red wine

SWEETNESS

Caramel, milk chocolate, vanilla, candy floss, honey

THE HISTORY OF
DISTILLING

Producing a spirit is pure alchemy:
the magical moment when water and alcohol
are separated through heat. So who came up with this
wonderful witchcraft? Good question. The history of
distillation has been written by everyone from scientists to
monks, doctors to traders, from every part of the world and
at every moment in history. As such, there is no defined,
authorized true biography of the process.

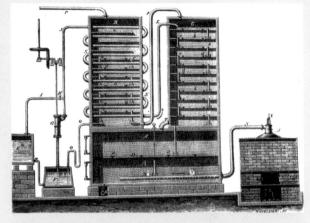

We do know distillation has roots as far back as the Bronze Age – probably in the Far East or Egypt – when the skills were used for medicine and perfume. But the idea of distilled spirit for consumption probably hit its stride in Europe around the 12th century. Wines were often distilled in an attempt to preserve them for long journeys, and as a result the first brandies became more readily available.

With the Black Death extending its velvet cloak of doom across Europe in the 14th century, many physicians turned to distilled spirits as a way to ward off the disease: the phrases *eau-de-vie* and *uisge beatha* – 'water of life' – were coined, and cereals, fruits and starchy vegetables began to form the basis of a spirit's recipe.

From the distillation of whisky in Ireland (alongside poitín – a raw, unaged, often potato-based spirit), gin in Holland, vodkas in both Poland and Russia, and schnapps in Germany, many other distinctly flavoured spirits followed, each relying as much on the personality of the producer as the availability of the base ingredient.

These early potable spirits, as well as medicine and perfumes, were predominantly made in pot stills which varied in size, shape and substance – from clay in Mexico, wooden in the Caribbean, to copper in Scotland.

↑ *The Coffey or 'Patent Still' changed the landscape of distillation.*

↙ *Distillation was very much a rural practice of necessity.*

But pot still distillation could only produce a limited amount of alcohol, often with wild variations between batches. The great shift comes in 1830, with the filing in Great Britain of Patent Number #5974 by a tenacious Irishman called Aeneas Coffey. His column still design enabled production at a faster and more consistent rate, giving rise to large distilleries around the world, as well as a completely neutral style of spirit.

Consider the column still as a motor car compared to a horse and cart. Whereas a rustic, more 'craft', made-in-batches approach was (and is) still very much at the heart of the production of spirits such as malt whisky, Tequila and brandy, the column still was continuous, churning out spirits in almost endless quantities.

Such was the revolution caused by Coffey's column still that in Scotland its use was challenged. Pot still whisky producers believed this tool did not create spirits in the same, well, *spirit* as the copper pots, and a Royal Commission to define 'what is whisky?' was commissioned in 1909 (see page 109). Coffey's still won the argument, and his invention continues to be used across the world for nearly every type of spirit.

Today, science has pushed the envelope further, with new techniques such as vacuum distillation (see page 17) leading to ever more precise spirit profiles. With such advances, the future of distillation looks intoxicating indeed.

THAT'S THE SPIRIT

THE PROCESS OF MAKING DISTILLED DRINKS

Before we go any further, a rather important definition.

Just what do we mean by **SPIRIT?**

A spirit is a distilled beverage with a significant level of alcohol, usually 25% alcohol by volume (ABV) or above. It is the product of a base ingredient, or ingredients, fermented to a low ABV (around 7–12%) which then has some of the water removed through distillation to increase the ABV or proof (see page 20).

Some spirits are bottled straight from the still (often with dilution); others go on to be matured in wood or other vessels.

Fermentation
This part of the process is the same as in beer-brewing or winemaking. The base product – grapes or grain, potatoes or plums; anything, really, that contains sugar or starch – is mixed with water and then with yeast, which breaks down the sugars into carbon dioxide and alcohol. In some circumstances the mixture is filtered before the yeast is added (Scotch whisky) and in others not (bourbon whiskey).

Typically, this will elicit a liquor of around 7–12% ABV, depending on both the length of fermentation, the activity of the yeast and the type of sugar in the base product: for example, sucrose, fructose or maltose.

The process of 'malting' is required with some cereals to help break down complex starch into simple, shorter chain sugars, and typically happens with barley. The barley is harvested and then tricked into germination – so it sprouts and grows – through a mixture of warmth and moisture. In doing so, it needs to release energy and thus breaks down the grain's inherent starches into sugars. Additional heat is then added to stop the process – heat that can sometimes come from burning peat, lending a distinct flavour to the final product (see pages 96–8) – and capture the now sugar-heavy 'malted barley'. These sugars are much easier for yeast to digest, and malted barley can be used as the whole ingredient (single malt whisky,

back into liquid as it arrives in the condenser. It is then stored separately in a spirit receiver, away from the remaining water and partial solids.

In pot stills (see page 13) the initial distillate will be somewhere around 20% ABV. Distil this distillate a second time and you can achieve a higher ABV of around 75%. Do it again, and you end up with an even higher, more purified spirit.

Distillers look to collect the most flavoursome part of a spirit run (often known as the 'heart') and separate out the unpleasant chemicals created by the process: congeners, methanol and other otherwise harmful elements. These are often known as the 'heads' and 'tails' of a spirit run. (See page 21 for a more detailed explanation.)

If you were to make the liquid work really hard, through a series of very small distillations, you can end up with a very pure spirit of up to 98% ABV.

for example) or as an additive to help kick start fermentation (in bourbon whiskey, for example). Some distilleries will activate the fermentation using a portion of the leftovers from the first stage of distilling. In bourbon production, this is known as 'sour mashing'.

Distillation

To bring this low ABV liquor up to spirit-strength requires the removal of water. Water boils (and thus turns into a gas) at 100°C (212°F) but alcohol has a lower boiling point, at just 78°C (172.4°F). A distiller takes the low ABV beverage resulting from fermentation and heats it to around 90°C (194°F). The alcohol turns into a vapour (evaporates) with the water staying as a liquid.

The next part of the distillation process involves capturing the evaporated alcohol and turning it back into a liquid. This is done using a condenser: traditionally a long pipe immersed in cold

water. This was once done with curled copper pipes, called 'worm tubs' or 'serpents'; these have been replaced by more modern versions called 'shell and tube' where a number of pipes are encased in a cold water jacket, quickly turning vapour

↑ *Traditional wooden washbacks for fermentation.*

↓ *Pot and column stills in use at Durham Distillery, North Carolina.*

STYLES OF
STILL

Pot Stills

Pot stills are the original means of distillation: essentially, copper kettles that funnel into a tight neck at the top, allowing for the alcohol vapours to be condensed and carried away to a spirit receiver. Copper is often the preferred material for two reasons: firstly, it is a malleable metal, which can be shaped into elaborate structures to aid distillation (most stills across Scotland are unique in style and, subsequently, spirit character) and secondly, it has active properties which help remove some of the heavier unwanted compounds and impurities.

In the early days, these items would have been small and portable, often used by farmers as an alternative use for produce. Now, pot stills are mostly static and used on a large scale globally – just one of the stills at the Midleton distillery in County Cork, Ireland, boasts a capacity of 80,000 litres…a little tricky to drag around on the back of a tractor.

Despite the large capacity of some pot stills and the distilleries which use them, they're considered a more artisanal method of distilling. This is partly due to their traditional nature and partly because distilleries that use pot stills produce their spirit in distinct batches. But the main reason they are considered 'artisanal' is in comparison to their industrial younger sibling, the column still.

Column Stills

Developed during the Industrial Revolution and often known as the Coffey still (see page 13) the column still (also known as the patent still and the continuous still) allows for huge volumes of alcohol to be manufactured from any base brew.

In short, these stills are designed to replicate heating and condensing of spirit a huge number of times in succession, eliminating the need for batches and creating a fast and continuous flow of alcohol. Distilleries with column stills

> ↑ *A more modern column still with windows to view the copper plates inside.*
>
> ← *A traditional copper 'alembic' still.*

dwarf their pot still relations in output. For example, the Cameronbridge Distillery in Scotland uses column stills to produce 100 million litres of grain whisky for some of the world's most well-known blends, and 40 million litres of alcohol destined for several best-selling vodka and gin brands.

Telling the difference between a pot still and a column still is easy: a copper pot still is like a small cottage in contrast to the immense skyscrapers of column stills, which are often so big that that they need to be situated on the outside of their production facilities, like a rocket ready to shoot into space at any moment.

Another key technique for distilling is cold or vacuum distillation. Rather than heat, pressure can be used to elicit an alcoholic vapour from the alcohol-water mix left after fermentation. The idea is that where the extreme heat of traditional distillation may damage the flavour compounds of the spirit, this ultra-modern style of distilling leaves all those delicate botanicals intact. It's particularly popular with smaller craft operations and can even be seen in a few hip bars.

In addition, retorts, doublers and thumpers are sometimes used: small chambers seen mostly in bourbon or rum production that create an additional 'super charger' condenser link in the chain, cleaning up the spirit even further.

MATURATION

Maturing is fundamental to the production of some spirits. Whisky, rum and Cognac are aged, often for decades, in predominantly oak casks to impart flavour and colour. Some Scotch whisky makers believe that as much as 70 per cent of the flavour and aroma of their product comes from the cask. In bourbon, where new oak casks are used, this impact is even greater.

How does maturation work? Let's look at whisky. Scotch and bourbon can only legally be matured in oak, which is a particularly porous wood, containing small veins. When it is filled with any substance, it soaks it up and retains a portion hidden in the wood.

For bourbon, only brand-new oak barrels are used. The oak inside is toasted or charred before being filled with high strength spirit, to allow phenolic substances (such as tannins and lignins) to be released.

Scotch and Irish whisk(e)y are matured in second hand casks, usually old bourbon or sherry casks. Occasionally casks that have previously held port, rum and red wine are used. Japanese Mizunara (a specific strain of oak, which grows in Asia) is also popular for certain high-end whiskies.

Know Your Wood: Different Sized Casks

QUARTER	BARREL	HOGSHEAD	PUNCHEON	PIPE	BUTT
125L	200L	250L	320L	480L	500L

When these casks are filled with high strength spirit, the liquid pulls flavour and colour from the oak: in the case of bourbon, that means heavy tannins and lignins from new oak. Scotch and Irish whisk(e)y get less oak influence and more of the flavours from the former occupant of the cask (port, sherry, bourbon). Each time a cask is used, it will impart less and less flavour to the spirit inside. Think of the cask like a tea bag or coffee grounds – each time you use it, the drink becomes weaker and weaker.

Oak also breathes, expanding and contracting with the temperature of the environment in which it is stored. This means that there is natural loss through evaporation, mostly of alcohol (although in some warmer, humid environments, water can be lost over alcohol). This loss is known as the 'angels' share'.

Over the course of 21 years, an average cask of maturing single malt Scotch will have lost a third of its contents. When distilling rum in warmer, tropical environments such as Barbados, the losses can run to as much as 12 per cent per year.

Another element to consider in the maturation process is the size of the casks used. The smaller the cask, the greater the surface area to spirit ratio and the faster and more intense the maturation will be. With wood maturation it is all about balance: too long in active casks and you'll get an astringent, bitter and undrinkable spirit; too short in active casks, and you might not even notice the influence of the cask. For some drinks, such as Cognac, you want to taste the grape spirit as the core, with minimal cask. In bourbon, spiced notes and vanillin from the oak complement the distinct flavours of the grains used in the spirit. This element of distilling and maturation, choosing which casks to use, looking after them, and ensuring they are used wisely, is known as 'wood management'.

SOME KEY WORDS
DISTILLERS

Can't Live Without

The art of distillation produces incredibly diverse results all over the world, despite the fundamental science behind the process being the same. Every distiller will have their trade secrets to creating a distinct recipe, but there's also a lexicon of words and phrases which are important across the whole industry. Here are some of the most important ones.

Alcohol:
Pretty straightforward, this. Without alcohol, we wouldn't have a distilled spirit as we know it.

- - - - - - - - - - - - - - - - -

ABV:
Alcohol By Volume. An accurate measure of the amount of alcohol in your glass.

- - - - - - - - - - - - - - - -

Condenser:
A vital piece of equipment that turns hot spirit vapour back into a clear liquid after it has been distilled. Usually seen partnered with a still.

- - - - - - - - - - - - - - - -

Consistency:
A term that can be taken two ways. Most distillers try to attain a consistent flavour profile in their bottlings, whereas others celebrate the inconsistency in flavour that comes from small batch releases, where the nuances change from batch to batch.

- - - - - - - - - - - - - - - -

Cut point:
The key moment when a distiller must begin to collect the desirable, flavoursome 'heart' of their spirit run.

- - - - - - - - - - - - - - - -

Distillate:
The liquid gold that every distiller lives and breathes for. It comes in thousands of styles, each one with its own spirited DNA – a personal statement from its maker.

- - - - - - - - - - - - - - - -

Duty:
A necessary evil. Every spirit will be taxed by the authorities and this tax is known as Duty.

Esters:
The building blocks of a spirit's flavour come from the array of chemical compounds produced during distillation. Esters provide the fruity, fragrant notes in a range of spirits – from whisky to brandy.

Ethanol:
This is the type of alcohol that can be consumed. Ethanol is the core of every spirit and the hero in the story.

Fermentation:
The all-important chemical reaction where yeast begins to consume the natural sugars in the mash of grain, molasses or wine, turning them into alcohol, which is then distilled.

Fusel oils:
The rather unpleasant alcohols that in large concentration can be harmful to the human body. In small amounts, they're likely to give you a hangover. The distiller's art is to discard these when they occur near to the end of a spirit run (see 'cut point').

Heads:
In a pot still set up, the 'heads' (or foreshots) are what first run from the still. They contain volatile alcohol compounds and the distiller separates them out from the quality 'heart' of the spirit run to be redistilled again.

License:
Look at the label on most whisky bottles and you'll see the word 'Established', followed by a date. Then change 'Established' for 'Got Caught'. Every legal distillery needs a license to distil.

Methanol:
Distillers really don't want much of this kind of alcohol in their spirit and aim to remove it during the process of making cut points. In large quantities, it will make you go blind or, at its very worst, prove fatal.

Proof:
A measure of the alcohol level in a spirit. The term relates back to when distillers would 'prove' the strength of their spirit by mixing it with gunpowder. If it still ignited, it passed the test. Today, it is simply double the ABV: a bottle of 80 proof vodka is 40% ABV, for example.

Reflux:
When a spirit is bubbling away in a still, the heavier, less desirable compounds have trouble making their way up the insides and fall back down. In essence, reflux adds to the purification of a spirit.

Still:
The centrepiece of every distillery. Pot stills made from copper are used around the world for whisky, brandy, Tequila and numerous other spirits. The column still (taller, more efficient pieces of equipment) allow the distiller to make much greater quantities of sprit in a shorter space of time and are used heavily in the production of vodka, grain whisky and rum. (See page 13 for more.)

Tails:
The last section of a spirit run which contains heavier, undesirable compounds. Separated out by the distiller and mixed with the heads, to be re-distilled again, in an effort to extract all the usable flavours from the spirit.

Temperature:
Get this wrong and your distillation won't happen: ergo, reason enough for distillers to get a very good thermometer.

Yeast:
Part of the Holy Trinity of fermentation, along with water and a base starch ingredient (grapes, grain, potatoes). Together, they form the heart of a spirit.

Yield:
Something all distillers have to consider: how to maximize the potential amount of alcohol they can produce from the raw materials they have. For example, a Tequila distiller will get just one litre of quality spirit from seven kilos of blue agave, the plant used in the spirit's production.

PART

TWO

Exploring the

WORLD OF SPIRITS

You've passed your technical know-how with flying colours – cheers to that! Now we can dive into the result of all that vapourising and maturing. This section of the book will examine the contrasting styles of spirits from all over the world, looking at the extraordinary diversity of character, cultures and people involved in the process. You'll find everything from absinthe to whisky, plus some wildcard spirits even a seasoned barfly might not recognize.

GIN

*a
botanical
bonanza*

GIN

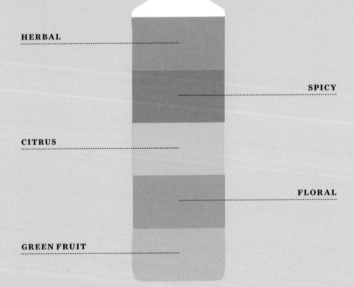

FLAVOUR & AROMA

HERBAL

SPICY

CITRUS

FLORAL

GREEN FRUIT

Gin is a gloriously free spirit. With a complex botanical heart, it has been an essential for the adventurous and the sophisticated for centuries. It has conquered continents, provoked a near ruinous period of British history and, in more recent times, reclaimed favour with an entirely new generation of drinker.

Today, gin is a global phenomenon, distilled and enjoyed in more than 70 countries with the Martini, Negroni and gin and tonic among the most well-known cocktails on the planet. Gin's newfound 'craft scene' has become the centre of huge experimentation too, with an explosion of locally grown botanicals, cask-ageing and flavours all pushing the boundaries of the spirit to new horizons.

But before we explore too far, let's first establish…

…WHAT IS GIN?

Gin is essentially a clear, neutral base spirit of no less than 96% ABV, either redistilled, compounded or flavour-enhanced with herbs, spices, citrus peels and other natural ingredients which can be fresh, dried or pre-extracted essential oils. This is then bottled at a minimum of 37.5% ABV under European Union regulations but can vary in strength when it is sold around the globe. In the US, the regulations are slightly different, with the base spirit a lower proof of 95% ABV. That single per cent difference actually adds flavour and aroma character to the resulting gin.

The single most important thing about gin, in our humble opinion, is that at its very heart must lie the juniper berry: the intensely herbal, pine-laden botanical (see page 35 for a more detailed description of this wondrous berry).

LONDON DRY

A City's Stamp of Approval?

It's at this point that the term 'London Dry' becomes important to understand. You'll have no doubt seen this stamped on the label of many fabulous traditional brands such as Beefeater and Tanqueray and perhaps wondered if this gives an indication as to where the gin is made.

London Dry is a bit of a misleading descriptor. In fact, London Dry gin can be made anywhere in the world, as long as it is made in the right way. All the botanicals are first steeped in alcohol so that the flavour compounds leech out. The alcohol is then redistilled, usually in a copper pot still, where the heady, botanical-heavy vapours are condensed back into the spirit. The distillate must be no lower than 70% ABV, with nothing added afterwards other than water – to dilute it to bottle strength – or additional neutral spirit to make that particular batch go further.

Some distillers like to place all their botanicals (more on these on page 39) straight into the base of the still, to help extract as much flavour as possible. Others, such as Bombay Sapphire, prefer to use what's called vapour infusion – especially for the more delicate botanicals, which would otherwise be cooked if boiled directly in alcohol. This process sees the botanicals placed in a copper basket riddled with holes, which fits into the neck of the still, to allow the alcohol vapour to pass through, extracting the flavours and aromas as it does.

Other Gin Styles Worth Noting

Next to London Dry, there is a vast range of other gin styles enjoyed globally.

DISTILLED GIN

Almost identical to London Dry (technically, London Dry is a style of distilled gin) but with the allowance of post-distillation additives, which can take the form of essential oils or single botanical distillates. Some distillers have made this a distinct feature: Hendrick's, for example, has a signature rose and cucumber aroma from essences added to the distilled gin.

COMPOUND GIN

A gin which takes a neutral base spirit and simply adds in the botanicals to give it flavour. It is the easiest way to make gin, given that all the heavy lifting is done by the process of infusion. During this process, some colour will seep into the spirit giving it a light, golden hue. After a few hours or days, the gin is ready. This style is known historically as 'bathtub gin', as it was popular in Prohibition-era America when people made their own booze at home by infusing spirit and flavours literally in the bath.

GENEVER

Legend has is that this is the OG gin. Genever, Jenever, or indeed simply 'Hollands' was a drink hugely popular in the Netherlands, which made its way across Europe and as far as the United States. A proportion of the base spirit – the 'malt wine', made from rye, corn and malted barley – is first double distilled to between 46–48% ABV. A proportion of this spirit is then distilled again with botanicals – juniper, hops and sometimes coriander – before it is blended back with the first spirit (sometimes it is cut with neutral spirit first) and then reduced down to around 38% ABV, dependent on the style. Genever often carries a particular savoury, malty, almost yeasty aroma, thanks to the base grains used in the malt wine. Three styles exist within the category. *Oude* must contain at least 15 per cent malt wine in addition to neutral spirit and must be bottled at no lower than

↗ *Dutch genever: the forefather of modern gin.*

30% ABV. *Jonge* must be no more than 15 per cent malt wine and bottled no lower than 30% ABV. *Corenwyn* or *Korenwijn* must be at least 51 per cent malt wine and bottled no lower than 38% ABV (some genevers are 100 per cent malt wine).

WACHOLDER AND STEINHAEGER

This German variant of gin (which translates literally as 'juniper') is commonly used as an umbrella term for numerous juniper-based spirits distilled in Germany, ostensibly in Westphalia and the Rhineland. Despite having been made since the early 19th century, this particularly juniper-heavy style of spirit, consumed as a chilled shot or a chaser, has remained a German favourite and is rarely seen internationally. Steinhaeger comes specifically from the Westphalia region of Steinhagen, which became protected under EU Geographical Indication regulations in 1989.

OLD TOM

A very traditional, slightly simpler take on gin, first popular in London in the late 17th and 18th centuries. Fewer key botanicals are used and the spirit is mixed with sugar syrup or honey to give a thicker, more viscous mouthfeel and sweeter taste, and arguably to mask its harshness. The Old Tom in question refers to the signage used by vendors back in the day, which depicted a cat. Despite

→ *Old Tom: a sweeter and more robust style of gin.*

its cruder origins, Old Tom has made a huge resurgence among today's craft distillers.

NAVY STRENGTH GIN

A style of gin that carries an alcohol content of 57% ABV (114 proof in the US) or higher, making it flammable. The name comes from spirits carried on naval ships: if the gin spilled, the gunpowder onboard would still be capable of igniting.

FRUIT AND SPICED GIN

This category was kicked off largely by the popularity of British sloe gin, where sloe berries are harvested, pricked and macerated in gin for a lengthy period of time before sugar is added. A veritable cornucopia of these macerated-style fruit gins exists around the globe, including citrus, strawberry, cherry, wine grapes (see page 45 for Australia's Four Pillars Bloody Shiraz gin) pear and plum gins, as well as styles containing spices such as saffron and vanilla.

COLOURED GIN

In addition to fruit gins, the popularity of coloured gins has really changed the landscape – also causing (not a little) division and derision among the purists! Pink gin was originally popularized by the Royal Navy in the 1800s, when a dash of bitters in the glass tickled

the gin pink. Today you can find a rainbow-hued fever dream of coloured gins, often with complementary fruit flavours added.

CASK-AGED GIN

The concept of cask-ageing isn't limited to the darker spirits of whisky, rum and brandy. A number of distillers have begun putting their finished gin in all sorts of different casks: French oak, American bourbon casks, ex-sherry casks and even barrels that previously held ginger beer. The maturation time tends to be a matter of weeks, rather than months or years, as the goal is to give the gin a slight flavour enhancement and more rounded mouthfeel, rather than a very wood-heavy finish.

A POTTED HISTORY

OF GIN

Gin has been on an epic 500 year journey of self-discovery and refinement before arriving as the clear, juniper-led spirit we know today.

The first mention of a juniper-based elixir was in a Dutch publication, *Der Naturen Bloeme* by Jacob van Maerlant in 1269, highlighting the medicinal benefits of a drink infused with the berry. However, it wasn't until 1495 that we have evidence of a juniper spirit being made, in a Dutch recipe for 'burned wine' (the term for a distilled spirit, which later became the basis for the term 'brandy', or fruit-wine distillate). This original recipe used a wine-base in which cardamom, cinnamon, cloves, galanga, ginger, grains of paradise, nutmeg and juniper were hot-infused, before the mixture was cut with either clean water or 'Hamburg beer'.

Distilled spirits became so popular in the Netherlands that in 1497 *korenbrandewijn* – a distillate from grain and the forerunner to genever – was designated as a taxable product. Throughout the 1500s, there are various mentions of *genever aqua vitae*, a grape brandy flavoured with juniper, and by the end of the century, grain-based spirits had become standard. In 1575, the Bulsius family set up the Bols Genever distillery in Amsterdam (see page 45) – now the oldest recorded spirits brand in the world. At the same time, an estimated 6,000 Flemish Protestants were making their way to London – due to religious turbulence in the Low Countries of Europe – taking a passion for juniper-flavoured spirits with them.

As trade routes around the world were established by nautical nations including Great Britain, France, Spain, Italy and Holland, it was the growth of the Dutch East India Company that provided a ready-made global distribution network for Dutch-made genever, while also bringing exotic herbs, spices and botanicals into the Netherlands. Distillers lost no time in experimenting.

Soon after, many British mercenaries went to fight in the Thirty Years War (1618–1648), and discovered genever worked rather well as fortification before battle, giving rise to the term 'Dutch courage' – still used today for those in need of a small motivational kick.

In 1688, the Dutchman William III became King of England and everything Dutch became fashionable. Londoners in particular turned their hand to making spirits flavoured with

juniper and other botanicals, which they named gin. Getting started was easy: in 1694, anyone who wished to distil simply needed to post a notice of intention outside their property, giving a fair warning of ten days, before starting up.

For those who couldn't be bothered with even this minimal red tape, a fashion emerged for a simpler undistilled gin. A neutral alcohol was simply put in a large container with juniper and other botanicals and left to infuse – helping to make the poorly produced base spirit palatable and giving rise to the term 'bathtub gin'. To make the drink more palatable, it was often sweetened, typically with honey due to the high cost of sugar at the time. It became known as 'Old Tom' gin (see page 30).

By the early 1700s, this homemade gin was causing serious problems in London. As the price of gin dipped below that of beer and ale, it became even more popular, especially with the poor. It is estimated that 50 million litres (or the equivalent of 90 bottles for every adult resident of the city) was being consumed per year at that time, and London's craze for gin – nicknamed 'mother's ruin' – was blamed for crime, madness,

sickness and child neglect. William Hogarth's *Gin Lane* (1750), one of the most famous artworks of the time, depicts the problem: a scene from the streets of London shows a community is ravaged by illness, hunger and death. Hogarth contrasts the engraving with another, *Beer Street* (1751), which shows men and women happy, jolly and full of life.

The Industrial Revolution of the early 1800s saw manufacturing of goods made immensely more efficient. The manufacture of gin wasn't exempt. With the development of the continuous or column still (see page 13) in 1831, quality neutral base spirit could be produced quickly and cheaply. Many of the famous gin brands we know today – Gordon's, Plymouth (page 44), Tanqueray and Beefeater – built a reputation on consistent quality.

Today, gin is produced on practically every corner of the globe. Each location puts its own inimitable stamp on the flavour and style of the spirit, but the tradition of a juniper-rich base remains a constant.

JUNIPER

Pungent Berry of Distilling Delight

At the heart of every gin is one particular botanical. The name needs little introduction to those who have enjoyed a gin before. But what is juniper, exactly, and why have distillers and consumers come to covet this tiny pearl of flavour?

The *juniperus* is part of the cypress family *Cupressaceae* and can be found growing widely in the Northern Hemisphere, in climates as diverse as the Arctic, the mountains of North America and the warmer climate of Southern Europe. Junipers are hardy evergreens, whose prickly green thorns have done little to stop those in pursuit of the unique aroma and flavour of its tiny dark 'berries' – actually small, deceptively fleshly 'cones' which bear a resemblance to embryonic pinecones. It is estimated that there are as many as 67 different varieties of juniper found growing globally, including *juniperus californica*, *juniperus deppeana* and *juniperus phoenicea*. *Juniperus communis* is the most widely used variety of juniper for gin.

Throughout history, juniper has been considered a remarkably valuable botanical. Legend has it that juniper was used as far back as 1500BC to treat ailments such as tapeworm, while documents dating back to 1055 reveal that Italian Benedictine monks were exploring juniper-infused tonics and ferments for their medicinal properties.

Harvesting juniper berries is done almost entirely by hand and is perhaps one of the most skilful, labour-intensive aspects of the gin-making process. This is due to the particular way the berries develop on the plant. Berries take two years to ripen and a bush will have many berries in varying stages of ripening. The branches cannot therefore be simply cut off and the ripe berries extracted. Instead, the bushes are beaten with sticks. Ripe cones heavy on the branch fall, while those growing stay safely on the plant until the following year. Once harvested, the distiller looks for the berries richest in the flavoursome essential oil.

CHARACTERISTICS OF JUNIPER

Juniper brings a herbal, pine-led note to a gin, with peppery, musky, resin aromas and flavours. At one extreme, it can be described as having petrol-like notes, or overly ripe tropical fruit such as mango and pineapple. The berries with higher oil content tend to come from plants grown in hotter climates, such as Italy and Southern European countries (Croatia and North Macedonia are both famous exporters of juniper).

THE REST OF THE BOTANICAL GANG

While juniper is the essential, dominant note within any gin, it would be a fairly one-sided affair without its supporting cast of botanicals. Some distillers like to focus on a core handful of well-rounded 'classic' botanicals which add depth, earthiness, spice and bitterness. These often include angelica root, cassia bark, orris, liquorice, ginger and coriander.

Once the foundations have been established, the distiller can accent each recipe however they please. They can add more spice in the form of peppercorns, clove, cardamom and star anise, for example. Fancy a more citrus-heavy gin? Add lemon, orange, lime and grapefruit peel. More floral? Introduce bergamot, elderflower and vanilla pods. Herbaceous? Olives, rosemary, celery, fennel and thyme are all popular additions.

To use a music analogy, each one of these key botanicals is a star performer, but perhaps too idiosyncratic and overpowering on their own. However, bring them together in harmony and you reveal a symphony of flavour.

Unusual Botanicals... the sky's the limit!

Some distillers like to produce gins which represent the landscape or terroir of the surroundings where the gin is distilled. Coastal distillers, for example, are known to add seaweed, samphire and even used oyster shells to bring a slight minerality and salinity to the resulting gin.

> ↑ *Aromatic botanicals give gin its rich depth and complexity.*
>
> → *Oily and herbal, juniper is the beating heart of every gin.*

Fresh or Dried?

When it comes to citrus fruit, the quantity of essential oil within the peel is key to how it reacts in a botanical recipe. Some distillers prefer using pre-dried, chopped peels which, when macerated in alcohol, distilled directly or vapour-infused, will release a more consistent result in the end product. Fresh peels contain more essential oils and are often bought in as whole fruits, before being hand peeled to preserve the fragrant, vibrant zing they give to the gin.

D.Blair ad nat. del. et lith.

M & N Hanhart imp.

JUNIPERUS COMMUNIS, *Linn.*

ENJOYING GIN

Gin's major asset as a world-class spirit is its versatility and broadness of flavour. While you'll find certain key classic botanicals used in the majority of gins, the beauty of this spirit is how easy it is for a distiller to tweak the recipe in a certain direction. To make sense of the infinite possibilities of gin, it is often categorized into flavour groups:

JUNIPER-FORWARD

Fewer botanicals, allowing the pungent, pine-led notes of the juniper berry to shine through.

Worth seeking out Sipsmith VJOP and No.3 London Dry (see page 45).

CITRUS-LED

More emphasis on the bittersweet aromas and flavours of fresh citrus fruit – lime and grapefruit are common, and exotic ones, such as Japanese yuzu, are becoming increasingly so.

Worth seeking out Malfy Gin and Nikka Coffey Gin.

SPICE-LED

Heavier emphasis on the drier, more aromatic spices, such as cardamom, clove and star anise.

Worth seeking out Ophir and Jaisalmer Gin.

FLORAL-LED

Slightly lighter and more delicate, floral-led gins are often graced with lavender, rose or elderflower, as well as some fresh orchard fruits.

Worth seeking out Warner's Elderflower Gin and Shortcross Gin.

HERBAL-LED

More savoury than the rest, with a heavy accent of fresh and dried herbs such as bay.

Worth seeking out Rutte Celery Gin and Gin Mare.

If you want to observe just how radically the addition of a few peppercorns or rose petals can alter a gin, we'd recommend a tasting with one gin from each of these styles. Begin by nosing or tasting them neat: that way, you'll begin to really get under the skin of each style and how they contrast to the next. Then try diluting them with a splash of tonic and note how they open up. Finally, try each one in a small G&T, with ice.

Joel & Neil's Perfect Serve

THE
MARTINEZ

Go to a cocktail bar and it's easy to be dazzled by the huge choice of gins. Any good bar should be able to recommend their favourite brand for a particular cocktail, the ingredients of which should accent a gin's botanical character. The most elegant and unfettered gin cocktail in this respect is the classic Gin Martini, humbly comprised of just two ingredients: two and a half parts gin and half a part dry vermouth, stirred over ice for 15 seconds until perfectly diluted (sorry Mr Bond, but a shaken Martini is a travesty to the senses...) The choice of gin is critical, as it is the main flavour in the glass. Our preference is something classic, with a solid mix of traditional botanicals, balanced citrus freshness, all underpinned by a bold juniper note. However, for a really out-of-this-world vehicle for your gin, look no further than the Martinez. Believed to be the precursor to the Martini, the Martinez brings all the vibrant citrus/juniper punch of its descendant, but with extra complexity and richness thrown into the mix.

HOW TO MAKE

MARASCHINO

VERMOUTH

BITTERS

BITTERS

GIN

* **TWO PARTS GIN (WE RECOMMEND NO.3 LONDON DRY GIN)**

* **ONE PART SWEET VERMOUTH**

* **ONE BAR-SPOON LUXARDO MARASCHINO LIQUEUR**

* **TWO DASHES ORANGE BITTERS**

* **ONE DASH ANGOSTURA BITTERS**

Add the ingredients to a mixing glass and half fill with ice. Stir for 15 seconds to dilute and chill the drink. Strain into a chilled coupe-style glass and garnish with a thin slice of orange zest.

MEET THE MAKER

}

Desmond Payne MBE

**MASTER DISTILLER EMERITUS,
BEEFEATER GIN**

Tell us what you do, Desmond.
I've been making gin for 50 years now. 'Watching the kettle boil' as I call it, which is what distilling really is! As Master Distiller at Beefeater in London, I wasn't allowed to make my own gin for 40 of those years. All I was doing was making James Burrough's Beefeater gin to his 150-year-old recipe, with a painting of him looking down as I devoutly and resolutely followed his original way.

What is the biggest challenge you face on a day-to-day basis?
Gin is based around the flavour of the juniper berry, the single most important ingredient we have. The juniper harvest is once a year and we buy all our juniper from Tuscany in Italy. This key ingredient is not cultivated. It grows wild. So the one thing we have to have, we have no control over. That means that when we buy, we must get consistent quality and style, because Beefeater gin must be consistent. Ensuring this each year is the most challenging part of my work.

How do you go about ensuring the consistency of the juniper?
We get in maybe 200 samples of juniper, from which we choose only four or five. This is done by assessment in our laboratory and some small-scale distillation, where we distil off the oils. Once we have the oils, we can make up some 'dummy' liquids. We line up 200 glasses

and nose them all. We call that 'The Big Juniper Sniff'! The juniper harvest is the most important time of the year; for me, no juniper, no gin. No gin, no job. No job, no money. No money, no gin. It goes full circle. So it is very, very important!

How do you drink gin at home?
My father was in the Indian Army. He told me he never really saw tonic water there, which dispels some of the myths as to what it was for, but they nearly all drank gin with a squeeze of lime. How do I drink my gin? It depends on the time of day and the mood I'm in, but you simply can't beat a good gin and tonic. It's one of those marriages that just works. And for a cocktail? At the moment, my favourite is a Negroni; a simple, no nonsense, grown up sort of a drink.

How do you make your G&T?
I don't like my gin and tonic packed with ice. I want to taste the gin. I certainly don't like the lemon garnish to be wrapped around the rim of the glass or squeezed and dropped into the drink. I place three lumps of ice into a rocks glass and add about 50ml – a decent measure – of Beefeater gin. To that I add an unflavoured tonic water in the ratio 3:1. That's three parts tonic to one part gin, not the other way round! Finally, a wedge of freshly cut lemon. No straw! I haven't needed to drink through a straw since I was seven.

10
ESSENTIAL GINS *TO TRY*

With its wonderful botanical balance and terrific versatility when it comes to serves, gin offers arguably one of the broadest flavour profiles in the spirits world. One thing's for sure though, you'll want to seek out a gin with a strongly beating heart of juniper for the ultimate experience. Here's our list of ten absolute classics, including beacons of the juniper berry and innovative game-changers, with which we urge you to get acquainted.

BEST IN GLASS «

» Plymouth
41.2% | Plymouth, UK
Also known as the Black Friars Distillery, Plymouth was established back in 1793, making it one of the oldest continuously run gin distilleries in the UK. Until recently, Plymouth was also the only UK gin to have a Protected Geographical Indication, meaning that under EU regulations, no other distiller could produce a 'Plymouth' style gin or indeed distil a gin in the town of Plymouth. Today's gin has seven botanicals – juniper, coriander, cardamom, orris root and angelica for an earthy note, plus two citrus peels – sweet orange and dried lemon. The juniper notes are soft but backed by a very balanced spice and earthiness, with a top note of fragrant sweet cardamom developing more strongly on the palate.

KEY

● WOODY	● SMOKY
● NUTTY	● GREEN FRUIT
● FLORAL	● RED FRUIT
● MINERAL	● HERBAL
● SWEETNESS	● SPICY
● FATTY	● CITRUS
● CEREAL	● VEGETAL

» No.3 London Dry
46% | London, UK
Berry Brothers and Rudd, the oldest spirits merchant in the world, are the noses behind No.3 – a favourite of the famous bar in Dukes hotel, London. This London Dry, actually made in Holland, is superb as a Martini gin with just six botanicals: juniper, orange peel, grapefruit peel, angelica root, coriander seed and cardamom.

» Roku
43% | Osaka, Japan
Roku brings together eight traditional botanicals with six uniquely Japanese botanicals: sakura flower and leaf, sencha and gyokuro teas, Sanshō pepper and yuzu. Each of the Japanese botanicals are harvested across four seasons to optimize extraction of flavour and ensure each ingredient is captured at its peak.

» Hernö London Dry
40.5% | Härnösand, Sweden
There are few awards Hernö, located on a small farm 260 miles from Stockholm, hasn't won for its extraordinary gins. Hernö is distilled with eight botanicals: juniper, cassia, lemon peel, vanilla, coriander, lingonberries, black pepper and meadowsweet. All are organic and the production is done by hand. A true Scandinavian gem!

» Bols Barrel-Aged Genever
42% | Amsterdam, Holland
Bols is arguably the genesis of modern gin. Its genever is built on a classic recipe, then a distillate of botanicals including coriander, star anise and aniseed is added. Finally, a malt wine spirit infused with juniper is added. Once these components are blended, the final mixture is left to mature in French oak casks for 18 months.

» Citadelle
44% | Cognac, France
Citadelle was conceived in 1996 in the most French fashion – over lunch on a sunny terrace at Château de Bonbonnet. Today the château-to-bottle Citadelle is produced on historic French Cognac stills and uses juniper grown on the estate, alongside 18 other botanicals including coriander, angelica and iris.

» Bluecoat
47% | Philadelphia, USA
Inspired by the rebels' uniforms during the American Revolution, Bluecoat celebrates the American spirit of independence. Launched in 2006, this American Dry Gin is made with 100 per cent organic botanicals. The exact recipe is a secret, but it does contain juniper, angelica, coriander seeds and a blend of citrus peels.

» Amázzoni
42% | Paraíba Valley, Brazil
Based in the verdant Paraíba Valley, around 130km from Rio de Janeiro, the Amázzoni distillery is a large, three hundred-year-old farm, recently restored to its 1717 pomp. The recipe combines pink pepper, laurel, lemon, tangerine, coriander and five Amazonian botanicals: cocoa; Brazilian chestnut; maxixe; victoria regia; and cipò cravo. A real taste sensation.

» Procera Blue Dot
44% | Nairobi, Kenya
Founded in 2017 by Guy Brennan, Procera is named for the specific kind of juniper in this gin, one which only grows 1,500m above sea level in the highlands of Ethiopia and Kenya. All the botanicals are taken from across Africa, including Swahili *ndimu* (limes) and pixie oranges from Kenya.

» Four Pillars Bloody Shiraz
37.8% | Yarra Valley, Australia
On its orchestra of stills, Four Pillars produces a 'Modern Australian' gin: designed to reflect the country's blend of cultures with European juniper, spices from Southeast Asia through to the Middle East, native botanicals and citrus from the Mediterranean. Bloody Shiraz also includes Yarra Valley Shiraz grapes, steeped in the gin for two months, giving a superb and uniquely fruity note.

RUM

sweetness & sunlight

RUM

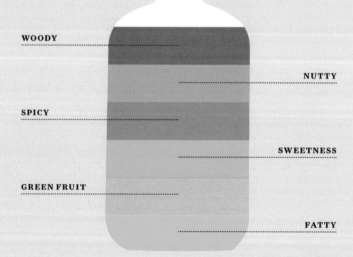

FLAVOUR & AROMA

WOODY

NUTTY

SPICY

SWEETNESS

GREEN FRUIT

FATTY

Rum is the diverse category of spirits, refusing to be pinned down by a simple definition. Beneath the veneer of those three simple letters is a world of radically different spirit styles, a vast array of sugars and sugar derivatives, many production methods and often esoteric local regulations.

Essentially, rum is a family tree and the lineage of each style can be traced back to the humble grass that is sugar cane (*Saccharum officinarum*). From here, it is very much a 'choose your own adventure story' as to whether the resulting spirit is made from the juice of the cane, the sugar itself or the by-products of sugar refinement (such as molasses). After that, there are the questions of how it is fermented, distilled, aged and blended.

This diverse family includes the bold, heavy, often aged rum made in Jamaica in pot stills (see page 13); the lighter, more earthy rhum agricole made in the French West Indies and on Réunion Island; and the complex aged and blended Cuban rum. The majority of rum is produced in the Caribbean and Latin America, the result of sugar cane plantations set up in the 17th century by European colonisers to feed the Western appetite for sugar. It's impossible to talk about the history of rum without acknowledging its roots in colonialism and slavery. Rum is essentially a by-product of these plantations, in which enslaved Africans and Indigenous people would labour in horrific conditions. While celebrating this fabulous spirit in its modern form – and its now-global nature – we think it's important to understand the darker practices in which rum's early incarnation are rooted.

Today, rum is made all over the world. It has nephews in Nottingham, uncles in the USA and aunts in Australia. It can be white, dark or golden; aged and spiced; cask strength, navy strength or overproof. Put simply, rum is a big old family, one known for its welcoming nature and warmth.

RUM

& THE HIGH SEAS

Rum is often associated with the navy, and was indeed the British Royal Navy's choice of liquor on long journeys across the high seas. Sailors were issued a daily ration of the stuff, known as a 'tot'.

The practice of pouring and drinking was known as 'totting' and was still very much part of the Royal Navy's way until 1970, when the final tot was poured and the ration cancelled. Occasionally, 'totting' will be revived, under the order of the monarch, or from a senior member of the Royal Navy, with an announcement to 'splice the mainbrace' – which actually means to repair a sail while at sea. This risky job earned the sailor tasked with its repair a befitting round of rum once completed. The motto remains in common parlance today.

Unsurprisingly, the cancellation of the daily rum ration did not receive a warm welcome. The day it was removed, 31 July 1970, was dubbed 'Black Tot Day' by Royal Navy sailors. This date is often used by rum producers to 'celebrate' the drink.

The term 'navy strength' obviously hails from the era of the nautical rum ration. Rums dubbed 'navy', 'navy strength' or 'naval' are not defined in law, but generally denote a style of barrel-aged rum, most likely from a former British colony such as Jamaica. They were stored on ship at a minimum ABV of 54.5% – compared to non-naval rum's typical 40%

↑ *Rum was once the lifeblood of the navy, with each sailor receiving a daily 'tot'.*

ABV. This strength ensured that any gun powder wetted by a leaky barrel would still ignite.

This strong, matured and highly flavoursome rum was the Royal Navy's standard tipple. Records show that until 1740, sailors were rationed half a pint, neat, of the spirit – twice a day. This was often laced with lime juice to ward off diseases such as scurvy: a heady blend that marked rum as *the* drink of the high seas.

STYLES OF RUM

Getting to the bottom of what makes rum *rum* is not easy, as it depends largely on local regulations (some legally binding, others far looser). Let's start with the basics: what you expect to see in a bottle marked 'rum' (see page 59 for 'How to Read a Rum Label').

WHITE OR LIGHT RUM

Clear rum is bottled straight from the still and only diluted with water. Some white rums are aged, but in very inactive casks, to minimise influence on flavour and colour. Other white rums are aged and have the colour removed through filtration.

GOLDEN RUM

Golden rum has no strict definition but has often been lightly aged for a few years in cask. Colour can also be added using caramel colouring.

DARK RUM

These rums have been aged for some time in the cask and carry the associated flavours of vanilla and oak. Typically, long aged rums are a heavier style of spirit that can withstand cask-ageing in a tropical environment. Be careful – some rums are artificially coloured to make them look as if they have been long aged.

SPICED RUM

Herbs, spices and other botanicals are added to rums such as Kraken and Captain Morgan, which are often designed for mixing.

COUNTRY FILE

There is a misconception that rum has no rules. While there are wild variations of style, and some countries indeed have no regulations on how this sugar-based spirit can be made, others have legally binding rules in place. Here we have an overview of three famous rum producing areas.

CUBA

Since 2013, Cuba has had a Protected Geographical Denomination (DOP) which sets the rules by which Cuban rum must be made. Firstly, the base product: Cuban rum is made from local molasses (also known as 'honey') and should be distilled in column stills (see page 13). Two different types of distillate are made thus. The first is called *aguardiente* and is distilled to around 75% ABV. This spirit is aged in oak for a minimum of two years, before being filtered through charcoal and blended with

↑ *Sugar cane fields in Cuba.*

the second style of distillate, known as *destilado de caña*, or *redistillado*, which has been distilled to a higher proof. The resulting blend, known as *ron fresco*, is then aged in oak casks, and the 'age statement' on the bottle is counted from the time this second maturation period begins. Some aged rums are re-casked for a third period of maturation.

JAMAICA

Jamaican rum is a defined and protected geographical indication (GI). The base can be sugar-cane molasses, the juice of sugar cane, crystallized cane sugar, sugar-cane syrup, or a combination of some or all of these. After fermentation, spirit can be produced in either pot or column stills. The pot stills must be copper, and the rectifier portion of the column still must be copper. The rum can either be bottled without ageing or aged in oak casks. If bottled with an age statement, the age must refer to the youngest rum in the blend.

> ↗ *A Jamaican sugar refinery.*
>
> ↓ *Rhum agricole: the traditional style of rum from Martinique.*

MARTINIQUE

The island of Martinique has its own AOC (*appellation d'origine contrôlée* – a controlled designation of origin) and strictly defined process for making rhum agricole. To be labeled 'AOC Martinique rhum agricole' the spirit can only be produced from cane grown in a certified area, and can only be made from fresh sugar-cane juice. No addition of syrup or molasses is allowed. Distillation must occur in column stills with particular specifications and should be between 65% ABV and 75% ABV for the final spirit. These rhum agricoles can be *blanc* (white rum) which must have been left to settle for at least three months, and not more than three months if aged in oak barrels; *elevé sous bois* (cask-aged rum) aged in oak barrels for at least one year; or *vieux* (extra-aged rum) aged in oak casks for at least three years.

Thanks to these differing regulations, the three regions produce radically different rums. In fact, the Cuban, Jamaican and Martinican rules are *much* more detailed than the headlines we have pulled out here. Rum is a very complicated world indeed.

PRODUCTION

Essentially, rum is made by fermenting and distilling either sugar, sugar-cane juice, or (mostly) molasses, the by-product of sugar production. Although there are also complex technical and legal processes in some countries and denominations, there are some basic principles we can use as a yardstick when it comes to understanding rum production.

The first is the base product: sugar, or sugar derivatives such as molasses or sugar-cane juice. Once you have chosen the starting point for your rum, the next stage is fermentation. Each style of rum will have different parameters here: different times, techniques and yeast types. Some use wild yeast, whereas others use specific local yeast strains. In Jamaica, distilleries employ 'dunder' – some of the leftover by-products from distilling rum. Dunder is added to the base molasses, helping to kick start the fermentation process, as well as adding additional 'funky' flavours typical to Jamaican rum.

Next up comes distillation. Rum can be distilled in either pot or column stills. The use of either type of still can have a huge impact on the final flavour and 'weight' of the rum. Traditionally, rums produced on column stills are lighter in character than those produced on pot stills, which tend to be bolder/oilier in profile. Some rum producers will use a retort, a small chamber between the still and the condenser, adding an extra layer of complexity and strength to the final spirit (see page 17).

Once the spirit is produced it can be bottled as white rum (see page 52) or casked for ageing. Ex-rum casks are highly prized by other spirit producers looking to add some zest to their products.

Cachaça

Cachaça is the Brazilian sugar-cane spirit, made in a similar way to rhum agricole. Until 2013, one of cachaça's main markets, the USA, called all cane sugar spirit 'rum'. Cachaça was no exception and therefore was labelled 'Brazilian rum' in the States. However, after much lobbying from both the cachaça producers and the Brazilian government, the law was finally changed to allow bottles produced in Brazil to carry the term cachaça.

By some distance the most popular spirit in Brazil today (helped by high import taxes on foreign spirits), cachaça also has a tragic history. Portuguese colonists in the 17th century used slave labour in the sugar cane plantations they set up to supply the West with sugar. From the fermented juice of this sugar cane, the Portuguese – already skilled distillers – found that a sweet, tasty spirit could be made.

Today, cachaça must legally be made from pure sugar-cane juice. The most prized are the artisanal offerings produced on small pot stills. It is a legal requirement to bottle the spirit between 38% and 48% ABV.

Like rum, cachaça can be both unaged (white) and aged in cask (gold). Casks can be made from a variety of woods, including native jequitibá, amburana and balsam. It is known as 'premium' cachaça if it has been 100 per cent cask-aged, and 'extra premium' if it has spent more than three years in cask. Cachaça is most famous outside of Brazil for being integral to the Caipirinha cocktail (mixed with sugar and fresh lime juice) which we personally feel is *the* way to enjoy this superb spirit.

OTHER CANE-BASED SPIRITS
OF NOTE

There are a number of sugar cane-based spirits across the world, which are a wider part of the rum family – distant cousins, if you will. Clairin, found in Haiti, is a distillate made from sugar-cane juice, sugar-cane syrup or a blend of both and is wild-fermented. Distilled in pot stills, it is not usually aged. Across India, Sri Lanka and Southeast Asia, arrack is produced from sugar cane and often the sap of coconut flowers. In Indonesia, Batavia arrack is distilled from a mix of rice and molasses and distilled in egg-shaped pot stills.

ENJOYING RUM

With such a spectrum of colours, textures and flavours, there is no wrong or right way to drink rum. Aged rums of real quality from places such as Jamaica, Barbados, Guyana and Cuba rival Cognac and whisky as serious sipping spirits. But of course, rum also lies at the heart of a fantastic array of classic cocktails: the Daiquiri, Mojito, Hurricane, Mai Tai, and the wonderfully rich Piña Colada.

HOW TO READ A
RUM LABEL

A rum label can contain an awful lot of information, from the country of origin to an age statement. Unlike the legal regulations for whisky (see page 104), where the age on a label must be the minimum age in the bottle, rum's age regulations vary by country.

BRAND

Often, many different brands are produced at a single distillery. Occasionally the brand name will simply be the individual distillery (if they make a single rum) but much like with bourbon whiskey (see page 106) you might have to work hard to find out who exactly has produced the rum.

COUNTRY OF ORIGIN

This is very important, as many countries – Cuba, Venezuela, Martinique, Guadeloupe, Jamaica, Réunion Island, Puerto Rico and Australia – have strict rules and regulations for their rum production.

AGE

Is the age on the bottle the youngest mature rum in a blend, an average age – or just a number chosen at random? Again, this will be rooted in the regulations of the country of origin.

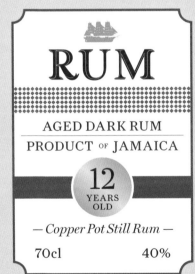

RUM

AGED DARK RUM

PRODUCT OF JAMAICA

12
YEARS
OLD

— *Copper Pot Still Rum* —

70cl   40%

AGEING

Some rums are only allowed to be matured in their country of origin. Others can be moved for maturation elsewhere.

STYLE

From a single distillery and pot still to a blended rum using column stills, some rum labels are keen to give you as much information as possible.

FLAVOUR

Depending on their country of origin, rums can have flavoured added and still meet the legal definition. You can find anything from simply 'spiced' through to 'pineapple', 'coconut' or even 'hemp'.

ABV

Legally all rum sold in the EU must be a minimum of 37.5% ABV. Navy strength rum will indicate that it is bottled at 57% ABV while 'overproof', such as that made by Wray & Nephew, is 63% ABV.

Joel & Neil's Perfect Serve

HOT PEANUT BUTTERED RUM

Many of the classic rum cocktails are long and refreshing and served over lots of ice. But rum can also be brilliant when served warm. This twist on the classic 'Hot Buttered Rum' has a nutty note and is perfect when the weather turns that little bit colder.

* **TWO PARTS DARK RUM**
* **TWO TEASPOONS RUNNY HONEY**
* **ONE TEASPOON SMOOTH PEANUT BUTTER**
* **4–5 PARTS HOT (NOT BOILING) WATER**

Mix the rum and honey in a jug until fully dissolved. Add the peanut butter and pour over a little of the hot water. Stir until melted, add the rest of the water then give a last quick stir and strain into a mug.

HOW TO MAKE

HOT
WATER

PEANUT BUTTER

HONEY

RUM

MEET THE MAKER

}

Trudiann Branker

MASTER BLENDER, MOUNT GAY RUM

Tell us what you do, Trudiann.
I've been the master blender at Mount Gay for the last four years. It's been the biggest change of mindsets for me. My background is in brewing and fermentation and then my world collided with spirits, where nosing, tasting, time and waiting are the most important things. It totally changed the way I work!

What's the biggest challenge you face on a day-to-day basis?
For me the biggest challenge is balancing the 'noise': it's easy to walk into the distillery to deal with a fermentation or distillation issue, or deal with maturing barrels, which comes naturally to me. To balance that with having time to think, brainstorm and allow your mind to go to a place where you can think about innovation – that lessening of the noise is the hardest part for me.

What's the secret behind creating a great rum recipe and what do you look for in Mount Gay?
I'll answer the second part first. You look for the traditional Mount Gay profile: vanilla, banana and dark chocolate.

You never look to create a blend the way your predecessor did. You need to look for the signature Mount Gay notes whenever you're putting a blend together. Within this, it's my interpretation of what those notes are: how big or how small, dependent on the distillation, maturation, age of the barrel and the type of spirit that went into it before. To do this I have to appreciate every part of the journey. For me, it's not just showing up at the end and putting it together. I like to be part of every stage: from understanding and choosing the molasses type, the length of fermentation, the cut points of the distillation and choosing the cask type. If you nurture every step and understand it, that's how to create the perfect blend.

How do you drink your rum at home?
Easy! Mount Gay XO with soda water and ice – no garnish.

Are there any great cocktails you have come across that have changed your perception of rum in mixed drinks?
When I became a master blender, I had to interact a lot more with mixologists and

bartenders and it blew my mind. I was so in my bubble making different rums and making them for all occasions, so to see how they were being used was very inspiring. I was in San Francisco in a lovely rooftop bar, and I had one cocktail handed to me: Mount Gay XO with a coconut water ice cube. I was like 'what is this magic?!' It was simple but amazing!

Finally, sum up Mount Gay in just three words.
Heritage. Blends. Heart.

10

ESSENTIAL RUMS TO TRY

With such a rich and diverse category, the question must be asked: what makes a good rum? Well, no matter if it is a clean and crisp white rum, an aged Cuban, or a funky Jamaican, it is all about balance and complexity. It needs to be neither too sweet nor too bitter, have good body and a decent ABV. You'll find that a good rum will accompany anything from a cigar to dessert and makes for an excellent aperitif.

BEST IN GLASS
«

» **Eminente Gran Reserva**
43.5% | Cuba
Gone are the days when just a single Cuban rum was available around the world. Now you can find several brands that work within Cuban guidelines to create and export excellent examples of the island's rum. Eminente is made using 80 per cent *aguardiente*, the lower proof, more flavoursome style of spirit (see page 54) with the rest of the blend coming from the lighter distillate. It is aged for ten years minimum and finished in French oak barrels. The rum carries a lightly fruity profile with notes of milk chocolate, rose water and black cherry.

KEY

● WOODY	● SMOKY
● NUTTY	● GREEN FRUIT
● FLORAL	● RED FRUIT
● MINERAL	● HERBAL
● SWEETNESS	● SPICY
● FATTY	● CITRUS
● CEREAL	● VEGETAL

» El Dorado Special Reserve 15-Year-Old
40% | Demerara, Guyana
El Dorado, famous for its three wooden stills, produces all the rum in Guyana at the Diamond estate. Its rum is made using locally sourced molasses from 100 per cent Demerara sugar. Coupled with the humid climate, this makes for a fast-maturing rum with a richness beyond its years.

» Leblon Reserva Especial Cachaça
40% | Minas Gerais, Brazil
Maison Leblon's co-founder and master distiller Gilles Merlet employs craft methods such as hand-harvesting sugar cane, with the juice used within three hours of pressing. This expression is aged for up to two years in French oak, giving it rich flavours of toasted oak alongside its cachaça heartbeat.

» Appleton Estate 12-Year-Old
43% | Santa Cruz, Jamaica
Created in the oldest Jamaican distillery with its own sugar cane estate and refinery, and distilled on both pot and column stills, this 12-year-old rum fares well with long ageing due to a large portion of each blend being from the pot stills. A wonderful mix of ginger cake, spiced pear, apricot and blood orange.

» Mount Gay Single Estate Series 01
55% | St Lucy, Barbados
One of the oldest distilleries in the world, Mount Gay's latest venture is a single estate rum that allows master blender Trudiann Branker (see page 62) to select molasses from different vintages. The first edition of this series was launched in 2023 and carries notes of mango, lime, sweet liquorice and vanilla tones.

» Planteray Stiggins' Fancy Pineapple
40% | Barbados
Flavoured rum is often seen as a gimmick, but Stiggins' Fancy Pineapple is taken very seriously. Named after the reverend, whose favourite drink was 'pineapple rum', from *The Pickwick Papers*, this is a blend of aged pineapple-infused rum and white rum redistilled with pineapple bark.

» Hampden Estate 8-Year-Old
46% | Wakefield, Jamaica
According to the distillery 'eight years in Jamaica in a tropical climate is equivalent to almost twenty-five years of maturation in the European climate'. This rum has no added sugar or flavouring and is a stellar example of high ester pot still rum with flavours of overripe banana, mango, vanilla, red apples, nutmeg and cinnamon.

» Veritas
47% | Jamaica and Barbados
Veritas (Latin for 'truth') is made from a blend of mostly unaged spirit made on column stills at Foursquare distillery in Barbados, and pot still rum from Hampden Estate in Jamaica. The result is a white rum that is textured and heavy yet highly mixable and flavoursome. A real treat for anyone looking to step up their white rum game.

» Flor de Caña 18-Year-Old
40% | Managua, Nicaragua
This distillery, one of few certified Fairtrade, is carbon neutral and family owned. Its rum is aged in white oak casks near the active San Cristóbal volcano, which sits just five miles away. The 18-year-old is rich and flavoursome with notes of honey, nuts and figs. A real winner of an aged rum, which works equally brilliantly as a sipping rum over ice as in a rum Old Fashioned.

» Trois Rivières Blanc
50% | Martinique
This edition really shows off how flavoursome rhum agricole can be. The original distillery closed in 2002 and Trois Rivières is now made at the island's La Mauny distillery, which has one column still dedicated to producing Trois Rivières spirit. Earthy, herbal and flinty in flavour, it has real personality and some great texture too.

TEQUILA

& the Agave Family

the humble herbaceous hermanos

*

TEQUILA

and the Agave Family

FLAVOUR & AROMA

VEGETAL

HERBAL

CITRUS

GREEN FRUIT

MINERAL

FATTY

SMOKY

Tequila – the talisman of the close-knit agave family – is possibly the most misrepresented category of spirit in the world. For decades, it was characterized by 'shot culture': a drink to slam at the start of an eventful evening, or the catalyst for descent into oblivion at the end of one.

Mercifully, this misalignment has become less of a distraction. Thanks to the likes of the late, great Tomas Estes (a truly pioneering educator, distiller and agave expert whose 2012 book, *The Tequila Ambassador,* set the bar for Tequila enthusiasts and frankly for all spirits communicators) the world has finally woken up to the extraordinary depth of flavour and quality the humble agave plant can bring to the table.

Bartenders around the world have shaped what was once a very limited palate of Tequila styles on the backbar into an extraordinary terroir-based map of Mexico. We're truly blessed that agave spirits are garnering so much attention from the industry. You might know mezcal (Tequila's smoke-laden cousin) but what about Sotol, Raicilla and Bacanora? These once seldom-seen or tasted Mexican spirits, which garnered little or no interest anywhere outside of the country, are now in the running to lead a whole new flavour revolution internationally. If ever there was a time to begin your agave journey, it's now.

AGAVE
HISTORY & ETYMOLOGY

Mexican spirits have an extraordinary deep-rooted, culture-shaping and life-affirming heritage. At the very heart lies the agave plant, or maguey, which has grown abundantly across the country since before the Aztec times – well over a thousand years ago.

Agave bears a striking resemblance to the aloe plant or the cactus, though neither is a direct relative. In fact, the agave plant – *Agavaceae*, to use its botanical name – is part of a family of succulents from which more than 200 varietals are thought to exist, growing in the southern states of the USA, Mexico and deep into south America as far as Venezuela. Varieties of agave are also found growing in India, particularly around the Deccan Plateau to the south of the Himalayas, which has led to some interesting spirits developing in the region, similar to Tequila in all but name.

This extraordinary plant thrives best in the trickiest of circumstances and locations. It has learned to overcome poor soil nutrition and a lack of moisture, which is why it was so vital to the Aztecs, who revered its moisture-rich heart and hardy, easy-to-weave strand-like outer leaves. Agave was a source of everything from food to textiles for the Aztecs. The sweet sap inside the plant's heart, or *piña* (named so because of the resemblance to a huge pineapple) was fermented into a cloudy, slightly sour-tasting drink called *pulque*. This was reverently reserved for religious festivals and sacrifices where the high priests would celebrate Mayahuel, the goddess of the maguey, believing the plant's sweet nectar to be the deity's lifeblood.

THE BIRTH OF MEXICAN DISTILLED SPIRITS

When Spanish conquistadors arrived in Mexico in 1521, they bought with them distillation knowledge and their challenge was to turn the traditional *pulque* into a spirit. Initially crude and harsh tasting, the conquistadors refined the process by turning directly to the agave plant. After stripping the leaves, the *piñas* were slowly cooked over fires, breaking down the heavy starches in the plant and allowing the natural sweetness to develop. The hearts were then crushed, fermented naturally and distilled, often in simple ceramic-based stills.

THE WHO'S WHO OF

AGAVE

...AND RELATED PLANTS

Scholars estimate that up to 40 different varietals of agave have been used to produce spirits, mostly in the mezcal category, such as Espadin and Tepeztate. Only one type is certified for Tequila production under Mexican law: the commercial benchmark Weber (Blue) Azul (see below). Each bottle of Tequila now sports a 'NOM code' which allows you to check via the website *knowyournom.com* at which distillery the Tequila has been produced.

There has recently been a groundswell of interest in wild agave (including the Tobalá varietal) which has a much smaller yield and takes far longer to mature than commercially grown plants. Each varietal, either wild or commercially cultivated, brings its own personality to the spirit into which it is eventually distilled, ranging from wonderfully light and floral notes to deeper dry, spicy aromas and flavour – just as grapes do for brandy (see page 131).

» **Weber (Blue) Azul** (from the species *Agave tequilana)*
The most commonly and commercially used variety of the agave plant is the gold standard in Tequila production, which was officially codified in 1977. It takes its name from the blue-grey leaves which can grow up to seven feet tall in fully mature plants. Weber Azul is a relatively quick growing variety, reaching maturity between five and nine years, dependent on the soil and growing conditions.

It favours the high altitude climate around Jalisco and Aguascalientes – the latter of which is around 2,000 metres above sea level. The flavours it brings are well-rounded, sweet and fresh, with fruity or slightly herbal notes.

» **Espadin** (from the species *Agave angustifolia)*
The most popular among mezcal producers, Espadin accounts for as much as 80–90 per cent of the spirit commercially available

→ *Highly prized wild-growing agave.*

↙ *Weber Azul: the key species in premium tequila.*

today. Its popularity is down to several defining factors: it's a relatively efficient varietal to grow, requiring around six to eight years to reach full maturity, and is less fibrous than other agave types, meaning it can be broken down fairly easily using either a Tahona or roller mill once it has been oven cooked. (See page 75 for more details.) Finally, it has a high inulin content (the natural starch required for conversion into alcohol) which gives a higher yield of spirit that's fresh, citrus and herbaceous in character.

» **Tobalá** (from the species *Agave potatorum*)
The jewel in the agave crown! Tobalá is a rare, difficult-to-grow variety, found in small pockets across Oaxaca and the surrounding areas of Guerrero, Michoacan and Puebla. As such, Tobalá mezcals – drier and earthier in style – tend to be very expensive and highly sought after. Unlike Espadin or more commercially viable agave plants, Tobalá cannot reproduce by itself and is reliant on birds (and sometimes bats) to help its seed proliferation. It is also both low yield, compared to Espadin, and slow growing, with some plants taking up to 15–16 years to fully mature.

» **Tepeztate** (from the species *Agave marmorata*)
A very special varietal. It can take up to 25 years for plants to reach full maturity, when vibrant bushy yellow flowers rise high out of the stem. Tepeztate is known for its highly flavourful, almost spicy character, which gives even greater intensity to the spirit.

» **Arroqueño** (from the species *Agave americana*)
The genetic mother of the Espadin variety, Arroqueño is a huge wild maguey plant, the leaves of which can reach over ten feet in width, and takes upwards of 20 years to reach maturity. It brings a bright and very green note to its distillate, with lighter floral overtones.

» **Pacifica** (from the species *Agave angustifolia*)
Also known as yaquina, this is a very specific agave type, reserved

for the production of Bacanora –the Mexican spirit which can only be produced in the foothills of the Sierra Madres in Sonora, to the far north of Mexico (see page 74). It has adapted incredibly to the difficult conditions and harsh terrain of the region and reaches maturity after around five years.

» **Dasylirion Wheeleri** (from the species *asparagaceae*)
Despite its visual similarities, the Dasylirion (more commonly known as the Desert Spoon) is unrelated to the agave plant, and is most commonly found growing in and around the city of Chihuahua, in the very north of Mexico. The plant is essential in the production of Sotol, another of Mexico's vibrant spirit categories which is very much on the rise (see page 86). Sotol has a particular herbaceous, almost pine-like notes with aromas of mint and eucalyptus.

TEQUILA

The Regions & Origins

Tequila production is split into several areas across Mexico: Jalisco, Tamaulipas, Guanajuato, Nayarit and Michoacán. Jalisco is by far the dominant force here, producing as much as 98 per cent of all the Tequila consumed globally. Jalisco is also geographically split into two contrasting styles: Lowland (or Tequila Valley) and Highland (Los Altos). The Lowlands are situated to the north and west of the city of Guadalajara, close to a dormant volcano, with a soil type said to produce more earthy, vegetal and herbal qualities in the agave grown there. The Highlands, located to the southeast of Guadalajara, have an iron-rich soil, which distillers believe brings out softer, more floral characteristics.

BACANORA
Sonora

SOTOL
Chihuahua, Durago, Coahuila

MEXCAL
Oaxaca, Guerrero, Durango, Michoacan, San Luis Potosi, Guanajuato, Tamaulipas, Zacatecas, Puebla

TEQUILA
Jalisco, Micohacan, Nayarit, Tamaulipas, Guanajuato

CHARANDA (A SUGAR CANE-BASED SPIRIT)
Micohoacan

RAICILLA
Jalisco

UNITED STATES

Gulf of Mexico

North Pacific Ocean

← *Jimadors stripping off the outer part of the agave.*

↓ *Agave piñas being loaded for processing.*

Tequila Production and Spirit Style

After the conquistadors' embryonic steps, Tequila production began to grow apace. The name Tequila may be used as an overall category descriptor, but it actually falls under the umbrella of mezcal (more on the specifics of mezcal later). Its spiritual home is the town of Tequila near Guadalajara in the state of Jalisco, established in the 17th century. The volcanic landscape was rich with the precious blue agave plants and it is now a protected industry, much like Cognac or Calvados. As its popularity grew, enduring brands came to life and the Sauza and Cuervo marques (Cuervo built the first licensed distillery in 1758) were among the first to export their spirits outside of Mexico.

Today, Tequila production is protected under a specific Mexican law: NOM-006-SCFI-201, which defines the techniques used to harvest,

ferment, distil, age and finally bottled the spirit. Two categories exist: 100 per cent agave style (more desirable and highly prized) and mixto, a 51 per cent agave base with a further 49 per cent of another spirit source – mostly found in the cheaper, less authentic products.

The agave *piñas* are hand harvested by the *jimadors*, who shed the outer layer of the plant using a special tool known as a *coa*, then loaded onto trucks which are taken to the distillery. There, they are cooked into sweet, fibrous flesh. This cooking, historically done in stone ovens, is now conducted in high pressure steam cookers or autoclaves, taking up to six hours to give the distiller the right consistency and sugar content. An even more efficient process of diffusion is used by some of the larger producers, whereby the sugary starches are treated with an acidic compound to separate out the heavier, fibrous starches from the required sugar-rich starch.

The more traditional oven method (still utilized by some of the smaller distillers) can take as long as four days. Traditionalists swear by the slower methods, feeling that rushing this important step can introduce an element of bitterness into the *mosto* – the name used for the fermented pre-distilled liquid. The average *piña* weighs 60–70kg and it takes as much as 7kg of processed agave to produce a single litre of spirit.

Once the agave has been cooked (creating an utterly delicious, honey-sweet material) it is time for the juice to be extracted for fermentation. Old-school and new-school

techniques are employed, each giving very different results in flavour and aroma. The Tahona wheel is the traditional method. This technique sees a huge stone wheel fixed onto a cross beam, which is slowly rotated around a shallow circular pit full of cooked agave. Historically the wheel was pulled by a donkey; latterly it has been mechanized. The modern roller mill has greatly sped up the processing time of this part of Tequila production. Some distillers feel that the slow, undulating manner of the Tahona wheel gives the juice a fuller, more

> ↑ *Small copper pot still production.*
> ← *The Siete Leguas tequila distillery, which uses traditional methods.*

rounded, thicker character to that of the more modern roller, which is said to give sharper, more citrus notes to the juice.

The juice is then turned into *mosto*: fermented with yeast and water to 5% ABV over a period of three to ten days, depending on temperature. The *mosto* is then distilled into *Tequila ordinario* – either twice in copper pot stills or once in larger, stainless steel column stills (see page 13) – to a strength of no more than 75% ABV. It is here that the true beauty of the raw spirit is unleashed: sweet, fresh, peppery and herbaceous notes are all in abundance in the new distillate. Recently, the Patrón distillery released El Cielo: distilled a radical four times, this Tequila retains the character of the spirit but has an incredible smoothness.

TEQUILA STYLES

Distillers can choose several pathways for their prized spirit

Blanco, or white Tequila

Also known as *plata* (silver) Tequila, this is simply diluted and bottled, usually around 40% ABV, without any ageing.

Reposado, or rested Tequila

A lightly aged version, with the Tequila matured in oak casks (usually made from American or French oak) for anywhere from two months to one year, giving a more rounded character and a slight golden hue.

Añejo, or aged Tequila

Reposado, but aged for up to three years, giving a much fuller, complex flavour, with more influence from the oak.

Extra Añejo, or extra aged Tequila

The pinnacle of maturation in the spirit. Held in oak for over three years, it develops bold, rich, buttery notes, spice and a sweet yet complex mouthfeel.

Cristalino, or filtered Tequila

A relatively new category, whereby an aged Tequila (usually *añejo*) has the colour removed from the final spirit by filtration, thus retaining all the character and mouthfeel that maturation brings but with the appearance of something altogether fresher and more youthful.

One seldom mentioned caveat is that by law, distillers can include additives (sweetener, glycerine or oak extracts) up to 1 per cent of the weight of the volume in the bottle, without needing to include any details on the label. While these additives are unlikely to majorly change the spirit we know and love, inevitably there's some enhancement. For a truly authentic experience, it is therefore worth exploring those brands vehemently against the practice. A useful website to check brands and additives, is *tasteTequila.com*, whose editors try and compile a list of additive-free brands and producers.

MEET THE MAKER

David Rodriguez

MASTER DISTILLER, PATRÓN TEQUILA

Tell us what you do, David.
I'm proud to say that I've been part of the Patrón *familia* for more than eighteen years. I'm honoured to have been given the opportunity to take over from the legendary [founding master distiller] Francisco Alcaraz and continue the legacy of the brand.

As Patrón Tequila's master distiller, I have a tireless dedication to perfection – that is at the core everything we do. I ensure that our *familia* continually goes to extraordinary lengths when executing our artisanal, handcrafted production process, ensuring perfection in every drop.

What's the biggest challenge you face on a day-to-day basis?
The craftsmanship, creativity and talent of the legendary Patrón production team has allowed us to constantly experiment, explore and create bold innovations while staying committed to our handcrafted production process and respecting the environment and community of our hometown in Atotonilco El Alto in Jalisco. With these values however comes great responsibility; standards to uphold and reputations to maintain which isn't always easy and is the main challenge of my role. For example, we must maintain the utmost respect for the agave we use. We only ever utilize properly matured 100 per cent Weber Blue agave plants. These are grown in the highlands of Jalisco and Guanajuato and are harvested at the optimal moment to maximize potential flavour. It's this craftsmanship and precision that yields a Tequila of the highest standard of quality.

What's the secret behind creating a great Tequila?
The secret is simple – Patrón Tequila does not compromise quality for efficiencies and is one of the only Tequila brands that has remained dedicated to a traditional, authentic, artisanal process since the brand's inception. No compromises, no cutting corners.

How do you drink Tequila at home?
My favourite at the moment is Patrón El Cielo. It's the first four-times distilled prestige Tequila and unlocks the natural sweet flavours of agave, delivering an incomparable taste with a bright, fresh and radiantly smooth finish. Best served on its own over ice, accompanied with a slice of the freshest orange you can find.

Finally, sum up Patrón in three simple words.
Innovative, handcrafted and passion.

MEZCAL

The Rustic Uncle of Tequila

Tequila's popularity is hardly surprising, given its versatility and utter deliciousness. The meteoric rise of its rustic, bold and altogether more sultry family member – mezcal – is less expected, though doubly exciting.

Mezcal brings a raw, unbridled charm to the party. Like that quiet friend, the thinker, often found sitting alone – who after a few drinks, opens up as a raconteur, bringing the room to life with their colourful tales and thrilling scrapes.

Historically, all Mexican agave spirits sat under the banner of mezcal, with Tequila effectively a type of mezcal produced in the town of the same name. However, Mexican law has tightened up the definition to highlight de-facto mezcal production in nine specific states of the country, with the largest and most significant of these being the farmland around Oaxaca, home to over 90 per cent of the mezcal distilleries. Thankfully, the rustic settings, traditional production techniques and centuries of skill that go into mezcal are now being shared with the rest of the world.

So Why the Smokiness?

It hasn't gone unnoticed that the smokiness in mezcal (we get a mixture of wood smoke and deeper, more herbaceous, almost agricultural aromas) bears some similarity to the smokiness of the whiskies produced on the island of Islay in Scotland. Mezcal develops its smoky flavour and aroma from the initial preparation of the agave *piñas*. Rather than cook them in steam-heated ovens, farmers dig deep pits, which are lined with firewood and stones, in which the *piñas* are slowly roasted for over eight hours.

Once the fires have died down, the pits are covered with the discarded fibrous leaves from the agave plants, tarpaulins and mountains of earth and the *piñas* sit slowly infusing with the oily, smoky residue of the ashes and coals for up to five days. Rather like the peat-smoked barley in a Scotch whisky, the smoke influence makes its way into the bottle. You'll find some mezcals have just a faint wisp of smoke while others offer a much heavier, bonfire note.

Wild Flavours…Wild Fermentation

Most artisanal small batch mezcals are fermented using the natural yeasts that live in the air around the distilleries. It is these strains that help influence the overall character of the spirit, depending on how effectively they turn all that sweet, smoky, starchy agave juice into alcohol. Traditional mezcals are fermented in the open air, sometimes for as long as 14–30 days, which can bring hints of overripe tropical fruit.

Does Mezcal Age at All?

A very contentious question! With agave spirits so popular, curious consumers are inevitably looking for unusual expressions. Traditional mezcal has almost always been bottled unaged, highlighting the specific flavours of not only the artisanal production but also the raw materials: all the different strains of often wild-growing agave. While a few mezcal brands rest their spirit in stainless steel to round off and marry the complex flavours, very few have committed to cask ageing, feeling that the oak overshadows the inherent flavour of the spirit.

← *A wide range of agave is used in mezcal production.*

↙ *The rustic craft in mezcal production remains largely unchanged.*

The Agave Stars of Mezcal

Not unlike grape varieties, different agaves make for fundamentally different mezcals. The terroir of the Mexican landscape (mountainous yet full of deep valleys), the soil type and hot conditions mean that certain agave types have become hardy and thrive in very difficult environments. Agave plants, including the commonly used Espadin (or sword variety, see page 72) are generally harvested after five to six years but certain strains, such as the wild Tobalá, grow erratically in more challenging soil conditions so require longer to mature. The longer an agave stays in the ground, the longer it is soaking up moisture, minerals and character, which is all abundant in the finished product.

Tradition and Flavour Bought to Life

One particularly beguiling aspect of mezcal is how it is entwined with Mexican symbolism. Take pechuga – a highly prized expression of mezcal, historically enjoyed at Mexican weddings. A selection of wild apples, plums, almonds, plantain and white rice is added to the still, alongside an already double-distilled mezcal. In addition to this, an uncooked chicken breast is suspended in the neck of the still, which the vapours of the newly distilled mezcal pass over, taking on a meaty note with wonderful fruity balance. Pechuga mezcals are hard to find and command a serious price but are absolutely worth exploring.

MEET
THE
MAKER

Eduardo Gomez

FOUNDER, OJO DE DIOS MEZCAL

Tell us a little bit about the concept of Ojo de Dios...
Ojo de Dios is the most innovative mezcal brand on the market. We decided to create a mezcal for everyone! Until now, mezcal was for very few people; mainly people from the drinks industry that understand booze. But the reality is that the regular drinker hasn't tried it, or if they have, the experience hasn't been the best. Most mezcals are super smoky and high in alcohol strength, which can be too much for many. Our Ojo de Dios Joven is smooth, elegant and delicate without losing the complexity of a good mezcal. And our other two lines, coffee and hibiscus mezcals, are world firsts! These are unique and more consumer-friendly than the standard mezcals. Both can be sipped neat but also make great cocktails.

What's the biggest challenge you face on a day-to-day basis?
Our biggest challenges have all been external. The global issues we have been facing in the last few years from Covid, economic and logistic crises, wars, the Suez Canal issue. For a period of time after Covid, it was impossible to get supplies, all factories were closed – so no bottles, no corks, no boxes. Those were very difficult times.

What's the secret behind creating a great mezcal? What do you look for in Ojo de Dios?
The secret is hard work and

respect. Hard work, because if you are an entrepreneur, you know how much work you have to do to build something up. It's 24/7 with no breaks, no holidays and no money, as you will need to continuously invest more and more. Respect, because you have to respect both the industry and your customers. We at Ojo de Dios take this very seriously, we respect the category of mezcal, we respect our producers and team in Mexico but we also respect our customers by offering the best possible product. No bullshit, no shortcuts!

How do you drink mezcal at home?
I love to drink Ojo de Dios Joven neat at room temperature, sip by sip. We say in Mexico that mezcal has to be kissed! However, I also make the best mezcal Tommy's Margarita, which is my favourite cocktail.

Any great cocktails you have come across which have changed your perception of how the mezcal category is evolving?
Ah, that's difficult as mezcal makes any classic cocktail better: Mezcal Negroni, Mezcal Espresso Martini, Mezcal Naked & Famous – all absolute fire!

Finally, sum up Ojo de Dios in just three words.
Innovation, quality and respect.

SOTOL, BACANORA & RAICILLA

The Next Wave of Agave Success…

With so much attention on Tequila, the huge pressures on the cultivation of Blue Weber agave and the rigorous restrictions which govern the regions it can be made in, distillers are turning to the wider portfolio of Mexican spirits. Mezcal has secured its place on the world stage – will Sotol, Bacanora and Raicilla be next?

Sotol is a fascinating diversion for the Tequila drinker, given that the two aren't really related at all. High in the north of Mexico, not far from the US border, lies the city of Chihuahua: home to Sotol. Instead of agave, Sotol is distilled from the Dasylirion wheeleri or Desert Spoon plant, another succulent shrub. Sotol has a herb driven, almost root-like spiciness to it. Its fortunes have recently been boosted by an unlikely ally: Lenny Kravitz. The rock musician partnered with a Sotol producer to create Nocheluna, one of the first brands to receive an international distribution.

Bacanora has been a closely guarded secret for decades and was actually illegal to produce until 1992. Since then, it has been granted a protected Denomination of Origin status strictly limiting its production to the state of Sonora, which borders the US state of Arizona. Bacanora can only be produced from the aquina or pacifica agave variety and utilizes the leaves and stems from the plant to give it a herbaceous, green, vegetal flavour and aroma.

Raicilla can only legally be produced in four regions: Sierra de Amula, Sierra Occidental, Costa Norte and Costa Sur. Given the wide diversity of terroir across these regions (both mountainous and coastal), the types of agave cultivated and differing production styles, Raicilla comes in a huge range of flavours: everything from sweet, grassy and floral to heavy, oily and smoke-driven. Raicilla is still fairly unknown outside of Mexico, but it's well worth seeking out as a fine example of how a craft-driven category can deliver such diversity of flavour.

Enjoying Agave Spirits

Put down the shot glass! The receptacle that led to Tequila's notoriety as a drink for downing in one and getting hammered on has done little to promote the wonderful, rich tapestry of flavour at the heart of well-made agave spirits. But look past the salt rims, lemon slices and bravado of old, and there's a world of unique experiences to be had. Sipping a neat glass of *extra añejo* evokes a moment of tranquil contemplation to rival that elicited by the best Cognac or single malt Scotch. Great agave spirits manage to perfectly integrate spirit character and traditional production techniques alongside oak-driven complexity.

Joel & Neil's Perfect Serve

FIRECRACKER
MARGARITA

The newly 'rediscovered' and reinvented classic cocktails such as the Margarita and Paloma are great places to start exploring different agave spirits. The Margarita's universal appeal as a smooth yet crisp, highly quaffable but very boozy drink can be given a real remix when bringing in a little chilli heat alongside your favourite silver (or *reposado*) Tequila. Likewise, start a party with a round of Palomas: fill a tall glass with ice, one part silver Tequila and a squeeze of fresh lime juice, topped up with pink grapefruit soda and a thin wedge of pink grapefruit to garnish. It will ensure top level soulfulness until the wee hours kick in.

HOW TO MAKE

AGAVE SYRUP

TRIPLE SEC

LIME JUICE

HOT SAUCE

* **TWO PARTS SILVER TEQUILA (WE RECOMMEND OCHO OR 1800 BLANCO)**

* **ONE PART LIME JUICE**

* **ONE PART TRIPLE SEC**

* **HALF PART AGAVE SYRUP (OR SUGAR SYRUP)**

* **DASH OF HOT SAUCE – TRY CHOLULA, TAPATIO OR VALENTINA MUY PICANTE**

TEQUILA

Add all the ingredients to a shaker with ice. Shake for 10–12 seconds and strain into a tumbler filled with more ice. Garnish with a sliced red chilli pepper, arranged to resemble devil horns.

10

ESSENTIAL AGAVE SPIRITS *TO TRY*

The diverse nature of the agave plant gives Tequila (and its relatives mezcal, Sotol and Bacanora) a broad spectrum of flavours and aromas: from heavy vegetal notes to rich, spicy, buttery and citrus led characteristics. Here's a selection which we feel represents not only the beauty of the plant, but also the extraordinary talents of the people who work with it.

BEST IN GLASS «

» Patrón Reposado
40% | Jalisco
Since its introduction back in 1989, Patrón has become the byword not only for quality, but also for enduring craftsmanship. Using both the traditional Tahona wheel and roller mill production, the unaged spirit is incredibly complex with bright, fresh vegetal notes, alongside a deeper, richer quality. This *reposado* expression raises the bar even further, with more than four months spent ageing in American oak whiskey barrels. Buttery, rich and complex, it has notes of vanilla and woody spice, alongside a hint of dried fruit and remnants of that distinctly bright, citrus-led freshness. This is superb enjoyed on its own over ice, or in a richer Paloma cocktail.

KEY

- ● WOODY
- ● NUTTY
- ● FLORAL
- ● MINERAL
- ● SWEETNESS
- ● FATTY
- ● CEREAL

- ● SMOKY
- ● GREEN FRUIT
- ● RED FRUIT
- ● HERBAL
- ● SPICY
- ● CITRUS
- ● VEGETAL

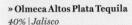

» Olmeca Altos Plata Tequila
40% | Jalisco
A major player in the world of Tequila and a real staple. The agave grows in volcanic, mineral rich soil in the Los Altos area of Jalisco, which sits around 2,100 feet above sea level. This silver (*plata*) expression has a herbal quality, with a bright and fresh citrus note, and works very well in a Margarita or Paloma cocktail.

» Tapatio Excelencia Gran Reserva Extra Añejo Tequila
40% | Jalisco
A masterpiece of a Tequila from the 'godfather' of agave, La Alteña's master distiller Carlos Camarena. This is rich and buttery, with a wonderful underlying spiced fruitiness from ageing in new French oak casks. Incredibly deep and resonant in flavour.

» Don Fulano 5-Year-Old Imperial Extra Añejo Tequila
40% | Jalisco
Produced by the legendary Fonseca family, owners of the La Tequileña distillery in Jalisco, this has been aged for five years (partly in Oloroso sherry casks) making it one of the older *extra añejos* out there. Rich, powerful and full of dried fruit and swathes of vanilla.

» 1800 Milenio Cristalino Tequila 38% | *Jalisco*
Owned by the same founders as the Jose Cuervo brand, 1800 is one of the fastest growing Tequila houses in the world. This *añejo* Tequila is matured in American and French oak and finished in port casks for a further six months, before filtration to remove its colour. Despite its clarity, it retains a smooth, unctuous mouthfeel and vibrancy.

» Ocho Blanco Tequila
40% | Jalisco
Another superb bottling, this silver Tequila possesses a deliciously clean palate, with notes of lime, some sweeter vegetal notes and a remarkable freshness, followed by a sprinkling of white pepper. Ocho is as versatile as Tequila can be: making a delectable Bloody Maria yet remaining smooth enough to sip as a palate cleanser.

» Ojo de Dios Hibiscus Mezcal
35% | Oaxaca
A relative newcomer, Ojo de Dios (see page 84) sources its seven-year-old Espadin agave from an estate in the mountains of San Luis del Rio. This fresh yet lightly smoky spirit is then infused with hibiscus flowers, handpicked from the coastal town, Rio Grande, and dried for 40 days, giving an intense berry ripeness and vibrant colour.

» Ilegal Joven Mezcal
40% | Oaxaca
Back in 2004, John Rexer began sourcing the best examples of mezcal he could find in Oaxaca to stock his bar, Café No Sé, in Guatemala. Today, as the founder of Ilegal, his eye and palate for a decent tipple remain undented. As with most mezcals, this is unaged and has some wonderful notes of medicinal smoke, peppercorns and cooked root vegetables, alongside toffee popcorn sweetness.

» Nocheluna Sotol
43% | Chihuahua
Sotol (see page 86) has been in the shadow of mezcal for many years due to a lack of commercially available brands. This is set to change thanks to a collaboration between Mexican spirits producers Casa Lumbre and rock music icon Lenny Kravitz. Nocheluna has a vibrant herbaceous aroma, with an underlying flavour of sweet grassiness and a touch of mint and eucalyptus.

» Aguamiel Bacanora
41% | Sonora
Bacanora (see page 86) is finally beginning to receive the attention it truly deserves. This example from Aguamiel has an earthy, dry smokiness up front, followed by a herbaceous, anise note and grassy flavours. An oddity for now, but a spirit which is only going to gain more global fans.

WHISKY

a
world
odyssey

WHISKY

FLAVOUR & AROMA

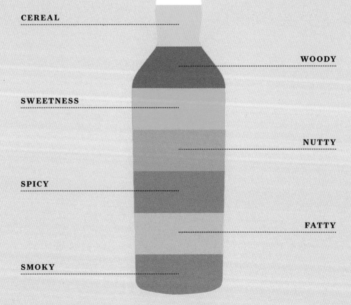

CEREAL

WOODY

SWEETNESS

NUTTY

SPICY

FATTY

SMOKY

Whisky is as much a status symbol as a drink. It has moved from a humble agricultural product into a serious sipping spirit, and an often incredibly expensive collectable one at that. But what exactly *is* whisky?

At its most basic, whisky is a family of distillates with cereal as the base product, with the most sought after made solely from malted barley. Distilled in small batches, it is then left to age in oak casks, often for a decade or more and occasionally into very old age, developing into the richly coloured and flavoured spirit we know today.

Scotland is synonymous with whisky, of course, and there is a common romantic perception of the world of whisky as a lone distiller in the Scottish mist, sampling a wee dram as stags roam about freely in the background.

But whisky is seriously big business. The bulk of it is driven by blended Scotch, Tennessee whiskey, Canadian whisky and some Indian brands that call themselves whisky but, due to global regulations, cannot be sold around the world as 'whisky'. All four of these styles can be told apart instantly in the glass, and even within Scotch there is a wide flavour spectrum, from light and spiritous to heavy and smoky.

If whisky is a language, each style produced by a country has its own local dialect; they are related but utterly distinct from each other. These international differences are rooted in the base cereal used, the production method and finally in the maturation environment of the resting spirit.

CEREALS

As with all spirits, the base product – here, cereals or grains – tends to be linked to what would have traditionally been farmed in the region around the distillery. However, there are some key cereals that make whisky, whisky – or indeed 'whiskey, whiskey'.

BARLEY

Barley is key to global whisky production. It is relatively easy to ferment, with the sugars hidden inside even easier to use after the process of malting (see page 14). Malted barley forms the base of single malt whisky but is also used in small portions in the fermentation of other grains such as wheat, rye and, in Ireland, unmalted barley.

There are two main styles of barley for brewing and distilling, named after the number of rows of kernels on each ear: two-row and six-row. Modern agriculture continually develops new strains which are easy to use and provide a high 'yield' of alcohol (that is, they have a good level of

sugar to enable yeast to covert it efficiently). There is an argument that these new strains prioritise yield over flavour, and some distillers are starting to use older 'heritage' strains in a

bid to drive more personality into the spirit.

Another property of barley is that it absorbs the flavour molecules of smoke if, during the malting process, the cereal is dried over burning peat. This lends a smokiness to the finished spirit, most famously in the malt whiskies produced on the Scottish island of Islay.

Single malt whisky is made from 100 per cent malted barley and is now made widely across the world. Some producers pride themselves on the use of home-grown barley, such as Paul John in India, who source six-row barley from the foothills of the Himalayas. Most distillers will simply use a commercial barley that gives a good yield and enables them to maintain their house style.

CORN

Corn (also known as maize) is widely used in the production of American and Canadian whisk(e)ys. It is also used in grain whisky (see page 99) an important part of blended Scotch. The corn is often pressure-cooked to release the starches, which are then fermented into alcohol with yeast, with a portion of malted barley added to kick start the process. One of corn's key properties is that it carries a sweetness to the final distillate.

↑ *Corn is a key cereal in the production of bourbon.*

↖ *Barley brings a malty richness to whisky.*

By law in America, bourbon whiskey must be made with at least 51 per cent corn. To be labelled as 'corn whisky' (for example the Mellow Corn brand) 80 per cent of the mash bill (see page 100) must be corn.

RYE

Rye brings a spicy, peppery note to a whiskey. There are some 100 percent ryes such as WhistlePig, which work wonderfully in a classic Manhattan cocktail, which originally called for rye whiskey as its base spirit. Today rye is also popular with European whisky distillers especially in Denmark and Finland (see page 123) where rye also grows abundantly – and now in Scotland too (see page 119).

WHEAT

Used mostly in American whiskey production, wheat imparts a mild, sweet, slightly nutty flavour and, as part of a mixed mash bill (see page 100) of other cereals, complements the more robust notes from other grains like corn or rye by softening the end result with more mellow characteristics.

OTHER GRAINS

Whisky can be made from many other cereals. Oats are used in some parts of the world, as are buckwheat, millet, spelt and rice (the latter in Japan). These produce unusual flavours which whisky drinkers might not associate with their favourite drink.

WHISKY STYLES

Single Malt

Single malt is *the* premium whisky style, owing to the artisanal nature of production. Just three ingredients are used – malted barley, water and yeast – and the spirit is produced in batches on copper pot stills (see page 13).

The barley can be malted (see page 14) using peat, which gives a particularly aromatic note when burned and can add an additional layer of flavour. The smoke level is measured in parts per million (PPM). The higher the number, the smokier the flavour. After distillation, the spirit is left to mature for at least three years in oak casks, and often for much longer.

> ↑ *The Ardbeg distillery on the isle of Islay: home to a rich, smoky single malt Scotch.*

The Scottish islands are famed for their smoky whisky-making, with Islay leading the way. The mainland regions of the Lowlands, Highlands and Speyside often don't use peat, and are thus known for a more delicate style of single malt. It's worth noting on a bottle's label whether a whisky is peated or unpeated, as smoky whisky is not to everyone's taste.

Across Scotland, and now around the world, there is a real drive towards single malt and each distillery has their own singular style. The 140-plus single malt distilleries are mostly there to feed the demand for blended Scotch (see below) and the master blender at any Scotch brand will ensure they have stocks from nearly all these distilleries at their disposal in order to create a consistent product, day in, day out.

Single malt whisky is not unique to Scotland, and the past decade has seen global growth in distilleries making whisky 'in the Scottish style'. Japan has long been a leading exponent of this style (see page 110) and quality single malt can be tasted from countries as far apart as Norway and New Zealand.

Grain Whisky

Grain whisky is produced at much larger facilities, on column or continuous stills (see page 13). The result is lighter and sweeter than malt whisky. Not as commonly available in bottle as single malt, single grain whisky is a workhorse: the vital component of Scotch blended whisky, which accounts for 92 per cent of the worldwide Scotch market. Despite this, there are just eight operational Scottish grain distilleries, compared to over 140 single malt operators. Grain whisky is mainly produced in countries that offer a blended whisky style, such as Scotland, Ireland and Japan.

Blended Whisky

Blended whisky simply means a combination of grain whisky and single malts. Famous names in blended Scotch include Johnnie Walker, Chivas Regal, Cutty Sark and Famous Grouse. All are huge global brands and have helped shape whisky's modern image. There is a real art to blending whiskies: not just in combining new products, but crucially in making big-selling brands consistent despite using whisky, from across Scotland's 150-odd malt and grain distilleries, which is subject to natural variations. Blending teams are highly trained to taste and test the new spirit before it enters cask and the maturing whiskies as they develop over time. Blends are predominantly made in Scotland, Canada, Ireland and Japan.

Bourbon

Bourbon, made across the USA, is distilled from a rudimentary beer made from a mixture of different grains, usually maize (corn) wheat, rye and malted barley. A minimum of 51 per cent must be corn, while no more than 15 per cent can be malted barley. This combination of cereals is known as the Mash Bill and, a little like a DNA strand, is different for each bourbon.

The standard formula is generally corn, rye and malted barley. 'Wheated' whiskeys (for example Maker's Mark) replaces the rye with wheat. All four grains can be used, but it is rare. If the rye content is over 51 per cent, the whiskey is no longer a bourbon but a rye. Many producers make both a bourbon and a rye under the same label (for example Michter's and Bulleit). Rye's

star has risen enormously since the turn of the century.

Bourbon grains are milled together and fermented before being distilled, often in a column still (see page 13) sometimes in a copper pot still (as at Woodford Reserve) and sometimes in a mixture of both. Occasionally a 'thumper' or a 'doubler' (see page 17) is used to give an extra level of distillation by producers who use a column still. Bourbon cannot exceed 80% ABV when distilled. Barrels must be filled with spirit no higher than 62.5% ABV. The minimum bottling strength is 40% ABV.

Once distilled, bourbon must be rested in brand new charred American oak casks, with no minimum length required. It can be labelled 'straight' if it has spent a minimum of two years in cask; if the label reads 'bottled in bond', the bourbon must have been aged for at least four years and bottled at 100 proof (50% ABV). It must also be the product of a single distiller at a single distillery, in one season (January to June, or July to December).

American Corn Whiskey

Made in a similar way to bourbon but from a minimum 80 per cent corn. It is not required to be aged in cask but if it is, new, uncharred oak or second hand oak barrels are used.

Tennessee Whiskey

The clue's in the name: this is only made in the state of Tennessee. The basic legal pillars of production are the same as bourbon, but Tennessee whiskey is either passed through maple charcoal before maturation starts or allowed to sit with the charcoal in a vat for a short period of time. This additional filtration element is known as the Lincoln County Process.

→ *Midleton distillery, Ireland: home to Redbreast and numerous other single pot still whiskeys.*

Canadian Whisky

Canadian whisky is made with a mixture of cereals which have been fermented, distilled and matured separately. Two main styles of distillate are produced: base (a highly rectified, lighter spirit used as the base for blending) and flavouring (a less rectified, heavier and more flavoursome spirit, where the flavour of each grain comes through more).

Maturation must be a minimum of three years in wood, and may contain up to 9.09 per cent added flavouring, as long it retains the style and characteristics of Canadian whisky. This additional flavouring can be Sherry, port, bourbon whiskey or even smoky Scotch, the latter used by the Wiser's brand in their 'Wiser's Union 52' edition.

Other styles

Rice whisky is produced mostly in Japan, and can also be found in other parts of Asia. In India, there are many bottles labelled 'whisky' which fall under the wider designation of 'Indian Made Foreign Liquor', or IMFL. It uses a base of neutral spirit often made from molasses which is then blended with grain or malt whisky imported from Scotland. The IMFL market in India is enormous, in fact, it's one of the largest spirits categories globally. However, neither IMFL nor rice whisky meet the legal criteria for products carrying the title 'whisky' in the EU or the USA. IMFL is not to be confused with genuine single malts (made in the 'Scottish style') from India such as Paul John and Amrut.

Pot Still Whiskey

A tradition of Ireland, single pot still whiskey was a solution to the taxation imposed on Ireland in 1682 (see page 112). It is made in very large copper pot stills using a mix of malted and unmalted barley at a ratio of about 20:80. The whiskey is triple distilled and aged for a minimum of three years in wooden casks, including American and European oak as well as some experimental varieties such as chestnut and cherry. The biggest exponent of this style is the Midleton distillery in County Cork, which produces such brands as Redbreast, Green Spot and Powers John's Lane.

The Magic of

MATURATION

TIME

One of the key features of whisky is the maturation in wooden casks. For bourbon it tends to be a minimum of – but not limited to – two years; for most whisky it is a minimum of three years, not just in keeping with the codes of production but in order to legally use the word 'whisky' on the label of a commercial product in the EU and UK.

TEMPERATURE

The very point of maturation is to bring colour and flavour to the whisky (for more on maturation see page 18). In Scotland, conditions are good for long maturation: the consistently low temperatures mean that the naturally occurring loss of spirit from the casks, known as the "angels' share", is small compared to other whisky-

producing countries. It is this slow maturation which gives Scotch a premium status within the whisky world. Right now across Scotland, around 20 million casks of whisky are maturing away, though not all will last into very old age. In fact, only a tiny percentage can retain sufficient volume of spirit (losses, not just from evaporation, are frequent) with enough energy and flavour (not becoming woody and astringent) to make it to three decades or more. This tiny percentage of exceptional casks command exceptional prices, which has led to an entirely new category of 'ultra-premium' Scotch that can cost the same as a super car or small house.

In the USA, bourbon producers have a different issue. The use of brand new oak casks means a more assertive maturation across whiskey-making states such as Kentucky, which are also far hotter and more humid than Scotland. The whiskey has to balance intense cask flavour as well as withstand temperatures that ramp up the maturation process. Some distilleries artificially heat their warehouses too, which enhances the interaction between the new oak casks and the spirit inside, speeding up the maturation. At the Bardstown Bourbon Company, huge glass windows have been used on one rickhouse to keep in the heat of the sun, allowing for a more natural warming of the casks.

CASK STYLE

Most single malt whisky producers around the world use second hand casks, often ones previously used to mature bourbon, Sherry, port or wines. Using an ex-Sherry cask gives the whisky a rich flavour of dried fruits; ex-bourbon casks traditionally impart vanilla and white flower notes to the spirit. Bourbon, with its fresh oak, gets really intense flavours of vanilla pods and tannic, dry wood spices. Grain whisky is predominantly matured in used bourbon barrels.

Japanese Mizunara oak has become a mark of Japanese whisky, particularly from the Suntory group, which used it in its single malts from Yamazaki and Hakushu, and the Hibiki blended whisky. Mizunara trees are short and curved, making it a particularly difficult oak to turn into casks, and as such the whisky from these rare casks is highly prized. Fewer than 400 Mizunara oak casks are produced each year.

CASK SIZE

Cask size is important (see page 19) and in Scotland no cask over 700 litres in capacity can be used to mature spirit. As whisky must be matured for a minimum of three years and a day to be called Scotch whisky, small casks would mean very fast maturation and most likely ruin a potential whisky before it was able to be christened with its true name.

A QUICK HISTORY OF
WHISKY-MAKING
IN...

...the USA

Bourbon's history, as with so much of American culture, was predominantly forged by European settlers, who brought the skills of distilling, a core part of agricultural life, across the Atlantic.

Many of the first settlers who were granted land to farm came from Scotland, Ireland and Wales, nations with a well-established history of whisky-making. A native Welshman called Evan Williams helped establish 'Bourbon Country' when he set up Kentucky's first distillery. The Evan Williams brand is now one of the world's biggest bourbon labels.

While it can be made anywhere across America, Kentucky has claimed the title as the home of Bourbon. The state's rich 'blue grass' farmland was ideal for growing the crops needed to make whiskey and the Mississippi

River provided the perfect route to the coast for exports to both America's big cities and overseas markets.

Ex-bourbon casks are now used across the world in the maturation of other styles of whisky and spirits such as rum.

Prohibition in the United States (1920-33) led to the closure of many distilleries (just six stayed open in Kentucky producing whiskey for 'medicinal purposes'), and a marked change in the landscape of American whiskey-making. It left just a few large producers to meet demand once the Act was repealed.

Today, bourbon production is alive and kicking once again with both small, artisanal pot still producers and larger facilities opening across Kentucky and the rest of America. In 2009, Kentucky was home to 19 distilleries. Today, there are 90 – and this number is only set to grow.

↑ *Prohibition sought to dismantle the liquor business in the US.*

← *Treasury agents ensuring every illicit drop was poured away!*

...Scotland

The history of Scotch whisky is one of a monk's medicine transformed into a huge global commodity. Documents from the 1494 Exchequer Rolls, held in Edinburgh's National Archives of Scotland, show an order from Friar John Cor for 'Eight bolls of malt wherewith to make aqua vitae.' That's enough malt to make many cases of whisky: clearly, whisky making was a legitimate business in the 15th century.

F ast forward 400 years and Scotch whisky making had become even bigger business. So big, in fact, that it was mostly made illicitly. This caused both public order issues and the Crown to miss out on huge tax revenues. Keen to see what all the fuss was about, King George IV went to Scotland in 1823 and demanded a glass of 'Glenlivet whisky'. The 'Glenlivet style' was a reference to the Highland and Speyside whiskies made in small batches in pot stills, often matured in transit before sale; a rudimentary version of what we would now call 'single malt Scotch'.

Soon after this royal tasting came laws: the 1823 Excise Act set a fee of £10 for licensing a

still and set duty rates. By 1824, a fair number of previously illicit whisky distillers had signed up to make their ventures legal.

In 1853 the blending of whiskies was made legal, with merchants and vintners realizing the appeal of a consistent product made from a variety of whiskies from across Scotland. Great examples were produced by the Walker family and the Chivas brothers, whose whiskies are still enjoyed around the world today.

The efficient Coffey still (see page 13) had been made available for distillers in 1830,

→ *Casks being transported manually by hand.*

↓ *A whisky bottling hall.*

↖ *Rural whisky making became a global industry.*

and by 1860 grain and malt could be legally blended. This process was not without controversy, with some producers challenging the very notion that grain whisky was indeed 'whisky' at all. In 1878, a group of Irish distillers – John Jameson & Sons, William Jameson & Co, John Power & Son, and George Roe & Co, all based in Dublin – published a book called *The Truths About*

Whisky claiming that Scottish grain whisky was 'evil'.

And so it was that in February 1908, the British government announced a 'Royal Commission on Whiskey and Other Potable Spirits', to ascertain the true definition of whisky. Ending in July 1909, the Commission found that any style of distillation could produce Scotch whisky.

Scotch has navigated legal battles, World Wars, Prohibition and fashion to come out on top. Today, blended Scotch still dominates the market (more than 92 per cent of Scotch sold worldwide is blended) but single malt has become the premium marque for the country's whisky output, and is globally recognized as the gold standard of malt whisky production.

...Japan

While Japanese distilled spirits have existed for centuries, whisky making is a relatively recent industry dating back just over a century, and is linked two visionaries: Masataka Taketsuru and Shinjiro Torii.

Taketsuru spent time in Scotland to learn the art of distillation, with stints at the Hazelburn distillery in Campbeltown on the west coast and at Longmorn in Speyside. He took the techniques and skills he'd learned back to his homeland and set up the very first Japanese whisky company. He joined forces with Shinjiro Torii, a successful local businessman and importer, and in 1923 the Yamazaki distillery was built in the Kansai plains, not far from the city of Kyoto. It was chosen because of the climatic conditions it shared with Scotland and also its abundant, clear mineral water from a site where three rivers converged, once home to a legendary 15th century tea house.

The whisky, while not an immediate success, was eventually very well received internationally, especially after the Second World War had ended. There are just under 30 working distilleries in Japan today. The major players are the Suntory Company, owners of the Yamazaki and Hakushu malt distilleries (the former famed for its lighter, more citrus led, vanilla-sweet style; the latter, its floral smokiness) and the Chita grain distillation facility; Nikka (a company which Taketsuru went on to found in 1934) which owns Yoichi (located in Hokkaido); and Miyagikyo in Sendai. These last two are both famed for their robust, fruity, spicy character.

Japanese single malt is a particularly limited – and thus very expensive – spirit. This was initially due to its domestic popularity and more recently thanks to its many awards, which truly opened the floodgates to international connoisseurs. Blended Japanese whisky is also a hugely popular style: the Hibiki blend (produced by Suntory, using a mixture of cask styles and spirit from the Yamazaki, Hakushu and Chita distilleries) is wonderful over a freshly carved ice ball in a tumbler and also as a classic Highball or Mizuwari cocktail, with beautifully clear ice and mineral water (see page 116 for our interpretation).

While the major players still dominate the industry, the number of internationally available craft operations has increased too, with the likes of Chichibu, a distillery established in 2008 in the Saitama Prefecture, and more recently Kanosuke in the Kagoshima Prefecture. Both of these micro-distilleries are beginning to make headway in the marketplace, despite being dwarfed by their peers.

Japanese whisky has been blighted by the rumours of imported whiskies being added to flagship blends. Until 1 April 2021, whisky of any origin, be it Scotch, Irish, Canadian or American, could be transported to Japan in bulk and effectively bottled as Japanese whisky, leading to a huge confusion and lack of transparency. Smaller companies both in Japan and Europe were also getting

↗ Traditional pagoda distillery roof in Japan.

↓ Kanosuke, one of Japan's newest distilleries, was opened in 2018.

↙ Shinjiro Torii, the founder of Suntory and the godfather of Japanese whisky.

in on the act, seizing on the prestige and scarcity of genuine Japanese whisky by putting inauthentic whisky in suitably Japanese-styled bottles with an impressive age statement, and selling them for grossly inflated prices.

As such, Japanese whisky producers came together to form the Japan Spirits & Liqueurs Makers Association (JSLMA) – a body representing the majority of Japanese distillers – to set out regulations for the production and labelling of Japanese whisky. Members including both the major players of Suntory and Asahi Breweries (the parent company of Nikka Whiskies) effectively define the term 'Japanese whisky', its production, bottling and labelling, acting as a firewall between those which are authentic and those pretending to be Japanese, in a business which, over the past decade, had become a grey and largely unregulated area.

Under the new guidelines, whisky labelled 'Japanese' must only use 'malted grains, other cereal grains and water extracted in Japan' as raw ingredients, while the fermentation and distillation 'must be carried out at a distillery in Japan'. The whisky must also be matured in wooden casks in Japan for a period of at least three years, much in-line with the minimum legal age of Scotch whisky.

Unlike heavily regulated and legally protected Scotch whisky, the new Japanese regulations and labelling standards are not law and only apply to members of the JSLMA. However, they are seen by the industry as a huge stepping stone towards a legally binding framework for all Japanese whisky distillers, bottlers and other independent companies involved in the export of whisky.

The Curious Case of

IRISH WHISKEY

Ask most people to name three countries that make whisky, and chances are you'll get Scotland, Ireland and America. America is famed for bourbon (see page 106) and Scotland of course for Scotch (see page 108). But it is Ireland that has experienced the most turbulence when it comes to maintaining its place in the world order of whisky.

In the late 19th and early 20th century, Ireland was a powerhouse of whiskey production, distilling one gallon in every seven made across Great Britain and Ireland. In 1871, the Distillers Company Ltd released a fundraising pitch for a potential new distillery in Dublin. Its text claimed that 'the demand for Dublin whiskey is estimated to be more than fivefold that of Scotch at present.' Yet by 1966 there were just two whiskey distilleries left in the Emerald Isle. What went wrong?

In the 1800s, Irish whiskey was largely produced in four big Dublin distilleries: William

Jameson & Co's Marrowbone Lane operation (later the Dublin Distillers Co); John Jameson & Son's Bow Street Distillery (home to the Jameson brand); George Roe & Co and John Power & Son. Just a handful of smaller distilleries operated around the rest of the country.

By contrast, 19th century Scotland relied on a of network of small, often rural distilleries (by the end of the century, it boasted more than 130).

Ireland's reliance on four large producers left its whiskey production exposed. Cold economic winds blew through the world of distilling in the first part of the 20th century, the result of huge oversupply, the Great Depression, World War I, and the onset of Prohibition in North America. The result was a downturn in demand for whiskey, which led to the closure of 40 Scottish distilleries. Ireland had to contend not only with the same bleak economic headwinds but with the 1916

Easter Rising and the 1922 Civil War.

Fast forward to 1960, and Ireland had lost 26 of its 30 operational distilleries, leaving just four: Bushmills in County Antrim, Northern Ireland; Jameson and Powers in Dublin; and Cork Distilleries Company in the south. The latter three merged in 1966 to form Irish Distillers, consolidating production at a new distillery in Midleton, County Cork, and leaving Dublin dry in terms of whiskey-making.

It wasn't until the end of the 20th century that demand really returned to the levels envisaged in the Dublin Distillers' pitch 150 years previously. By 2015, whiskey was once again being made in Dublin, with Teeling the first whiskey-distilling operation to open in the city for 40 years. Ireland now boasts over 40 whiskey distilleries, and this is growing all the time. From single pot still (see page 13) through to single malt, column and blended Irish whiskey (see page 99), Ireland is back at the top of its whiskey-making game.

Enjoying Whisky

The age-old question of how to drink whisky is as delicate as the question of football team affiliations in a Glasgow bar. Differences of opinions abound, and strong ones at that. However, the reality is that most master blenders of any whisky style will dilute their samples down to around 20% ABV (by adding the same amount of water to whisky). In other words, adding water is fine! Ice will chill and slightly 'numb' the whisky, while adding dilution at a slower rate as the ice melts. If a whisky is 'cask strength' or 'barrel proof' – that is, bottled directly from the barrel or cask with no dilution – the strength is likely to be quite high. If this is the case, it is worth adding water bit by bit, tasting as you go, to achieve a result pleasing to your palate.

Of course, drinking whisky 'neat' – enjoying it straight out of the bottle – is a fantastic experience. However, whisky of all dominations can be enjoyed as a mixed drink too. In Japan, it is often served poured over crystal clear ice with equally high-quality spring water, in what's known either as a Highball (with sparkling water) or Mizuwari (with still water).

In the USA, signature drinks for bourbon include the Mint Julep (nearly 120,000 are served each year across the two days of the Kentucky Derby), Old Fashioned, Whiskey Sour and Manhattan.

Scotch works well in a Highball, but is also at the heart of drinks such as the Rusty Nail, Bobby Burns and the Penicillin, this last using heavily peated Scotch. In other words, there's really no wrong way to drink your whisky.

Joel & Neil's Perfect Serve

WHISKY HIGHBALL

Inspired by trips to Japan, this cocktail is a refreshing mix of either a great blended Scotch or Japanese whisky and soda water, with a crack of black pepper and lemon peel.

* **TWO PARTS SCOTCH WHISKY (BLENDED WORKS PERFECTLY HERE: LOOK OUT FOR ARDRAY, A BLENDED SCOTCH FROM SUNTORY)**

* **FIVE PARTS SPARKLING WATER**

* **FRESH CRACKED BLACK PEPPER**

* **LEMON PEEL, TO GARNISH**

Add the whisky to a tall Highball glass. Add some ice and soda and stir. Then add more ice and soda until the glass is full. Use a pepper grinder to add black pepper on top, and garnish with lemon peel.

HOW TO MAKE

BLACK PEPPER

SODA
WATER

WHISKY

MEET THE MAKER

Kirsty Black

MASTER DISTILLER, ARBIKIE DISTILLERS

Tell us what you do, Kirsty.
I run the production side of Arbikie Distillery. We're a field-to-bottle distillery and a small team so we all contribute to all aspects of distillery operations. This means on any given day I can be working on what crops we want to grow next, mashing in [the first stage of whisky-making], tasting our maturing stock or doing the regulatory reports.

I've always enjoyed solving problems and figuring out how things work. I think that this has always been at the heart of everything I've done – both in my hobbies and at work. Although I started out studying plant science and working in a maltings [malt house, where grain is malted – see page 14] during the holidays, it took another ten years and a career working in medical devices before I ended up here at Arbikie. The major change happened when I decided to take a year out and complete a masters in brewing and distilling at Heriot-Watt University. Here I crossed paths with the Stirling family and, as they say, the rest is history!

What's the biggest challenge you face on a day-to-day basis?
The biggest challenge is also what I like the most about working at Arbikie and that's the variation. Every day sees something different. This does mean, however, that you need to be able to wear a lot of hats and generally there's not enough hours in the day!

What's the secret behind creating a great rye?
For us it's the amount of control we have and care we take through every step of the process. By growing our own raw materials, we are really connected to them – we see the seasonal and varietal differences and how that translates to the spirit we put into casks. We want to take as much care in the distillery as the farm team has during the growing season and hopefully that comes through in the spirits we release.

How do you drink your whisky at home?
That's a tricky one – it really depends on my mood, the weather and the company! I like my whisky as a straight dram as much as I do in a cocktail. I'm a big fan of the classics, so you'll often find me with a Boulevardier, an Old Fashioned or a Highball.

Any great cocktails you have come across, which have changed your perception of whisky in mixed drinks?
I've always been a fan of whisky cocktails so don't think I needed my perception changed. I think that's one of the good things about us at Arbikie – although we respect the history and traditions of whisky making in Scotland, we come from a mix of backgrounds, so we approach making spirits (and drinking them!) with fresh eyes and no preconceived ideas.

Finally, sum up Arbikie in just three words.
Innovative. Sustainable. Exciting.

MEET THE MAKER

Rob Samuels

MANAGING DIRECTOR, MAKER'S MARK

Tell us what you do, Rob.
I'm Rob Samuels, eighth generation whisky maker of the Samuels family and grandson of the founders of Maker's Mark.

What's the biggest challenge you face on a day-to-day basis?
As a global brand with demand that continues to grow, it's tempting to consider how to change the way you operate to be more efficient or to capitalize on quick-win opportunities. Resisting those temptations is a challenge, but it's something that is very important to us at Maker's Mark.

When my grandparents founded Maker's Mark in 1953, they didn't do it with the intention to be the biggest brand or the most commercially successful. They did it to create a bourbon that they were proud to share with their friends and their community. It's my job and my privilege to honour their legacy by keeping their vision at the heart of everything we do today and everything we're building for the long-term future. To me that means being committed to quality and consistency in the whisky we craft for our fans; being purposeful with exciting innovation that's grounded in our founders' taste vision; being stewards of nature and our communities; and creating a great culture for our team.

What's the secret behind a great bourbon recipe?
Crafting a great bourbon comes down to three things. First, starting with flavour in mind. When my grandparents burned the 170-year-old family recipe that had been handed down to them, it's because they knew what they did not want in a whisky. They had a specific vision of a bourbon that was soft and smooth, with no bitterness. They crafted Maker's Mark to meet this vision, choosing to use red winter wheat instead of the traditional choice of rye as a flavouring grain.

Second would be the quality of ingredients. Bourbon is nature distilled, so it's important to us that we are stewards of our land and natural resources. As a certified B Corp, we are always looking for ways to give back more to our natural environment than we take, while crafting the most flavourful bourbon possible.

Finally, it's important to be consistent. I'm proud that the Maker's Mark our fans enjoy today is made in the same fashion as the very first bottles that my grandparents shared with their family and friends in the 1950s.

How do you prefer to drink bourbon at home?
I prefer Maker's Mark neat or with just a little ice. Maker's Mark Cask Strength is my personal favourite.

Are there any great bourbon cocktails you would recommend?
Our signature serve for Maker's Mark is The Gold Rush, which is a riff on a whisky sour that substitutes honey syrup for simple syrup: 2 parts Maker's Mark, ¾ part honey syrup and ¾ part fresh squeezed lemon juice, with a lemon wedge to garnish.

Sum up Maker's Mark in three simple words.
Flavour-forward. Handmade.

10

ESSENTIAL WHISKIES TO TRY

Of all the dark spirits, whisky – whether Scotch, American, Irish, Japanese or hailing from any number of other countries – surely offers drinkers the widest variety of flavours and styles by which to be enraptured. Cask maturation has a great deal of influence, but it's not simply the case of 'oldest is best' – there must be genuine spirit character too.

KEY

- WOODY
- NUTTY
- FLORAL
- MINERAL
- SWEETNESS
- FATTY
- CEREAL
- SMOKY
- GREEN FRUIT
- RED FRUIT
- HERBAL
- SPICY
- CITRUS
- VEGETAL

BEST SINGLE MALT IN GLASS »

» Glenmorangie Signet
46% | Highlands, Scotland
A unique single malt whisky from Highland distiller Glenmorangie, long celebrated for its light, easy going, well-rounded whisky, that's full of fresh citrus and soft vanilla notes. Signet, first created as an experiment in 2012, is an extraordinary sidestep in terms of flavour. At its heart lies a heavily roasted chocolate malt spirit, which brings deep notes of dark chocolate, espresso and bonfire toffee. A masterpiece of distilling and a genuine delight for the senses.

BEST BLENDED IN GLASS »

» Hibiki Japanese Harmony
43% | Osaka, Japan
A remarkable layered, complex blend, bursting with zestiness. Hibiki has been a game-changing blended whisky since first coming to prominence in 1989. This latest iteration combines different styles of single malt whiskies from Suntory's Yamazaki and Hakushu distilleries with grain whisky from the Chita distillery, matured in a varying number of cask types including Japanese Mizunara oak.

» Tamdhu 15 Years Old
46% | Speyside, Scotland
A Speyside gem which is rapidly becoming the industry insider's favourite dram. Founded in 1897, Tamdhu is exclusively matured in Oloroso Sherry casks, which are made from a mixture of American and European oak. This makes for a perfect balance of buttery, vanilla-led sweetness and rich, spicy, dried fruitiness.

» Four Roses Single Barrel
50% | Kentucky, USA
A bourbon with a well-rounded character. The distillery, led by master distiller Brent Elliott, uses two separate mash bills and five different yeast strains to create a wide variety of flavour, from delicate fruit and floral notes through to slight spice and rich fruit. Aged for up to nine years in the Kentucky heat, this is complex and yet wonderfully approachable at the same time.

» Wire Works Caduro
46.8% | Derbyshire, England
The White Peak distillery in Derbyshire was founded back in 2016 by Max and Claire Vaughan in an abandoned Victorian industrial building. Its whisky, Wire Works, is a rich, unctuous and delicious dram that has won fans the world over for a vintage style not often found in modern day whisky. This is a future classic.

» InchDairnie RyeLaw
62.5% | Fife, Scotland
Ian Palmer of InchDairnie distillery is the Wonka of whisky, constantly turning ideas into reality in his innovative Highland distillery. Everything about InchDairnie is about moving Scotch forward as a category, and its RyeLaw expression is the first whisky in the world to be made using malted rye, distilled in an unusual Lomond still. Its taste is as remarkable as it is innovative.

» Thomson South Island Peat
46% | Riverhead, New Zealand
The reputation of Australian whisky is flourishing thanks to the likes of Starward, Lark and Sullivan's Cove. So too is its neighbouring Antipodean distillers, notably Cardrona and this absolute gem from Thomson, located to the northwest of Auckland. It is distilled using locally grown barley and smoked over peat cut on the South Island. The result? A fresh, vibrant and totally idiosyncratic whisky.

» Kyrö Rye
47.2% | South Ostrobothnia, Finland
Heavily inspired by the national pastime of sauna culture, the founders of Kyro have an uncanny knack of producing world class spirits, presumably in the most relaxed fashion possible. The central building block to all Kyro's whiskies is rye, which grows abundantly across Finland. This wood smoked version, using alderwood, is every bit as vibrant as it is laid back. Relax and ponder existence.

» Method & Madness Japanese Chestnut Cask
51.8% | Cork, Ireland
The premise of Method & Madness is as theoretically sound as it is utterly bonkers. Produced at the Midleton distillery in Cork, it is a collection of highly unusual cask finishes, grain types and other distilling magic, bringing a touch of madness to the resulting whiskey. This chestnut cask is full of floral freshness, with a darker, sweeter nut-laden richness in tow.

» Paul John Bold
46% | Goa, India
India, despite being arguably the biggest consumer of 'whisky' (see page 103) has very few traditionally focused single malt distilleries. However, the major players – Rampur, Amrut and Paul John – are producing truly world class spirits. Paul John Bold is exactly what it says on the bottle: a wonderfully rich, smoky and bold expression, yet surprisingly easy to drink.

FRENCH BRANDY

a divine trinity

✻

FRENCH BRANDY

Cognac, Armagnac & Calvados

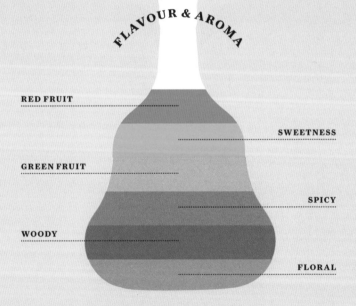

FLAVOUR & AROMA

RED FRUIT

SWEETNESS

GREEN FRUIT

SPICY

WOODY

FLORAL

France is famous for not one, not two but three spirits, all of which are protected in their production methods and the regions in which they can be produced.

Cognac

Ask most people for a French spirit, and they'll probably say Cognac. This particular style of grape brandy has worked hard over centuries to establish itself as one of the most premium spirits in the world, an effort supported by major houses such as Rémy Martin, Martell and market leader Hennessy.

Armagnac

Made in the Gascony region, Armagnac hasn't historically had big brands going into battle for what is a fundamentally agricultural product. Often made on mobile stills for a few days a year by small, artisanal, farmhouse producers, this grape-based drink nonetheless carries bags of flavour and personality and sells more in its native home than Cognac.

Cavados

Calvados is the odd one out. Where its cousins Cognac and Armagnac are made from grapes, Calvados is produced from apples and pears. That certainly doesn't make it any less tasty, and it's the world's leading form of 'cider brandy'.

COGNAC

France's Most Regal Spirit

The town of Cognac is about an hour's drive northwest of Bordeaux. Like the Mississippi in Kentucky, the Charente river which snakes through the town provided a vital trading route for the distilleries of the region, creating a direct link to the coastal ports and onward to the rest of the world.

The Cognac region is the second largest grape growing region in France. Its wines are known for their high acidity and challenging flavour as a table wine, hence their reappropriation for brandy as far back as the 1400s. But it was in the 1600s that the product became more refined and commercially successful. Producers began to practice the art of double distillation, first filling their alembic stills (see page 132) with wine, then redistilling the first run of the spirit to obtain an additional level of rectification. The result was a spirit with a higher alcoholic content that retained a lot of grape flavour.

As the spirit was transported first down the Charente, and then on long journeys by sea, the oak casks used to store the spirit began to have an impact on the flavour. With a growing popularity in the members' clubs of London, Cognac was transported in cask to Bristol, where it was left to mature further before heading east.

↗ *Grapes are the lifeblood of Cognac production.*

→ *Jarnac – the heart of the Cognac region, on the banks of the River Charente.*

A variation on this practice, known as 'early landed', is still in use today.

Cognac's rise in popularity hit a bump in the road in the late 19th century, when French vines were blighted by an outbreak of the particularly troublesome Phylloxera bug. Wreaking havoc through Europe's vineyards, the result was a contraction in the supply of all grape-based products, and a golden opportunity for Scotch and Irish whiskey to fill the void.

Today's thirst for Cognac has been supported by major brands who act as blending houses. In the region there are more than 3,500 grape growers and 1,500

distillers. These small producers sell their spirits to the likes of Martell and Hennessy who age and finally blend them for their signature house styles.

The Cognac industry is a big presence within the spirits world. Global powerhouses produce millions of bottles a year. However, there are still plenty of single estates across the region, essentially small landowners, farmers and distillers producing very limited quantities of spirit, which rarely see the light of day outside of the Cognac region.

The Importance of Terroir

The French are vigilant about protecting their own products and in 1909 the Cognac region became what's known as a 'Demarcated Area', with strict regulations on how and where Cognac can be made. This legislation is rooted in the region's terroir; the soil in which the key grape varieties used in Cognac are grown.

T he most sought-after grapes are from the Grande and Petite Champagne areas. Located in the middle of the region, these are home to chalky soils, similar to those in the Champagne region, hence the name. Vines grown here produce grapes with a complex flavour which can age well in the cask. If a Cognac is labelled as Fine Champagne, it is a blend of spirits from both Grande and Petite grapes, with a minimum of 50 per cent coming from the Grande *cru*.

Borderies is a small area to the northwest, adjacent to the two Champagne regions. The soil here is clay-heavy, bringing a nutty note to the finished spirit that is famed for long ageing.

Fin Bois is the largest region by area and produces the most Cognac. As such, quality varies, but this area can produce exceptional grapes for great distillation.

Grapes from the Bon Bois and Bois Ordinaire (an area that extends to the northwest of France) produce much lighter style spirits that don't tend to age well and lack complexity compared to the other regions.

> ↗ *The neatly arranged grape vines in the Grande Champagne region of Cognac.*
>
> → *Ugni Blanc grapes provide the perfect balance of acidity and sweetness.*

GRAPE VARIETIES

Cognac is made from a variety of white grapes, each of which has a huge impact on the overall flavour of the finished spirit. The grape varieties are set in law (currently eight are allowed, although more are being trialled due to the effects of global warming on the sugar content of the current crop) and the majority of wine is produced from just three main grapes.

UGNI BLANC
(or Trebbiano)

Makes up 98 per cent of all grapes planted in the Cognac region. Ugni Blanc has a good balance of acidity and sugar and is rather hardy and resilient. Known for maturing well in oak.

FOLLE BLANCHE
(Picpoule)

Harder to grow but brings a lightness of touch and a delicate flavour to the spirit. Fewer than one per cent of all grapes grown in the region are Folle Blanche.

COLOMBARD

Another minority variety but still key for bringing a floral and fruity dimension to Cognac. Despite being known as hard to grow and for lower yields, it is still very much part of this trinity of varieties. One of the oldest continually grown grapes in the region.

OTHERS

At least 90 per cent of the grape spirit used to make Cognac must come from the three grapes mentioned here. If the blender so chooses, the other 10 per cent can come from grape varieties such as Sémillon, Montils, Folignan and Meslier Saint-François.

Making
COGNAC

The starting point, of course, is grapes: white grapes are harvested around August, September and November, and turned into wine. This wine cannot be stored for long, and no preservative sulphites are allowed. Legally, the wine must be distilled before 31 March on the year following harvest.

The wine is then fed into a copper alembic pot still (also known as the Charentais still) for a double distillation method that takes the wine from around 10% ABV, to a spirit of 68–72% ABV. Once the spirit, known as eau-de-vie until it has aged sufficiently to be called Cognac, emerges from the still as a clear liquor, it goes into oak casks.

These casks are made from French oak, grown in either the Limousin or Tronçais forests. To be legally called Cognac, it must rest in these casks for a minimum of two years, but often is left for much, much longer. Rather confusingly, the 'age statement' on a bottle of

↑ *Hennessy Cognac maturation cellar.*

Cognac (see opposite) tops out at XO, or ten years old, but plenty of XO Cognacs contain liquid that has matured for many generations.

Casks made from the fine-grained Sessile oak tree grown in Tronçais tend to give an aromatic, slightly less tannic note to the maturing spirit, whereas Limousin Pedunculate oak trees have a wider grain and allow the spirit to soak deep into the staves, extracting a dryer, oaky character over time.

As it ages, Cognac develops rich spice and leather notes, followed by the fabled 'rancio' note, which often comes across as truffle or mushroom. These Cognacs are highly sought after. It's important that Cognac does not become *too* oaky, however, and for there to be a balance between grape and oak. As such, once a Cognac hits perfect maturation in cask, it can be moved to glass demijohns or 'bon bons'.

Walk through a maturation cellar in the Cognac region and you'll pass by some casks that are ageing nicely. Wander a little further and you'll come across 'Le Paradis': the magical room full of true alchemic delights. Here sit demijohns of all sizes containing very old and rare Cognacs, some dating back to before the Phylloxera bug took its toll, and quite possibly containing grape varieties that no longer exist.

Classifying Cognac

Developed in 1865 by Maurice Hennessy and today regulated by the BNIC (Bureau National Interprofessionnel du Cognac), the labelling on a Cognac bottle is key to understanding the age and complexity of the spirit.

VS: VERY SPECIAL
Matured in oak for a minimum of two years.

VSOP: VERY SUPERIOR OLD PALE
Matured in oak for a minimum of four years.

XO: EXTRA OLD
The youngest eau-de-vie must be at least ten years old, but the Cognac will often contain older spirit upwards of twenty years.

NAPOLEON
Usually means a spirit somewhere between the XO and VSOP age ranges.

Other distinctions such as 'Vieille Reserve' and 'Hors d'âge' are often used to describe Cognacs beyond the XO category and are typically of exceptional age and quality.

MEET THE MAKER

Patrice Piveteau

CELLAR MASTER, COGNAC FRAPIN

Tell us a little bit about yourself and your role, Patrice.

I have worked for Frapin for 32 years. First and foremost, my job is to maintain the quality of the Cognac. This quality is linked to not just the ageing but the terroir, the vinification, the distillation – so I need to take care of these elements too. I also have to manage the stock to ensure we have enough to produce VSOP or XO. The last part is to be an ambassador of the brand.

What's the biggest challenge you face on a day-to-day basis?

The biggest challenge is to continue the quality of the Cognac Frapin day after day!

What's the secret behind creating a great Cognac and what do you look for in Frapin?

There is no secret, it is due to our terroir, our know-how and a long time…No recipe.

In Frapin, I look for a longer finish, finesse, aromatic richness, elegance and complexity.

How do you drink Cognac at home?

It depends on the moment. It can be as a cocktail or neat as an aperitif. It could accompany

a meal through a food-pairing experience, or be enjoyed neat as a digestif. I am nothing if not flexible!

Are there any great cocktails you have come across, which have changed your perception of how the Cognac category is evolving?

Cognac in cocktails was not trendy 30 years ago. Today it is. I like an Old Fashioned best because it is not too sweet, there is a good balance and we still find the Cognac taste within it.

Finally, sum up Frapin in just three words.

Terroir, know-how, quality (and history, if I can be permitted to use four words)!

ARMAGNAC

The Definition
of a Craft Spirit

From country to country, continent to continent, there are three words which spirits enthusiasts can seemingly no longer escape: Artisanal. Craftsmanship. Heritage.

These words have been long overused by copywriters from some of the world's biggest spirits companies in an attempt to give personality to their wares in an industry which fundamentally prizes consistency.

But take a trip to a particularly tiny area of France, and you'll find one spirit that truly embodies those overused words. It's a spirit that has refused to be pigeonholed for more than 700 years. Armagnac is not *a* craft spirit. It is *the* craft spirit.

Still very much a French brandy, Armagnac is often overshadowed by its better known sibling Cognac. Both grape distillates are from France; in fact most similarities, especially in the final product, come from their similar base ingredients.

Armagnac is not only the oldest brandy to be produced in France, it's the oldest recorded spirit in the world. This noble brandy can trace its roots back to the 14th century, with its fabled medicinal properties listed in a 1310 document (now a highly prized literary treasure in the Vatican) by Prior Vital du Four, a Franciscan theologian, who later became a cardinal. In it, he claimed Armagnac had 'Forty Virtues', including 'rendering men joyous, preserves youth and retards senility. And when retained in the mouth, it loosens the tongue and emboldens the wit, if someone timid from time to time himself permits'.

ARMAGNAC
RYST
"de Haut Parage"
CONDOM ★ GERS

THE KEY DIFFERENCES

Armagnac & Cognac

Visit the Armagnac region of Gascony, 250km south of Cognac, at distillation time and you can witness the ancient ritual of the lighting of the stills. Many Armagnac producers grow their own grapes and produce their own wine, but not many own their own stills.

A more rustic style of still is used for Armagnac than for Cognac. The Alambic Armagnacais is a small continuous or column still, made of three parts. There is the column part itself, which sits on a small boiler (either gas-fired or occasionally directly wood-fired) and houses a number of distillation plates, over which the spirit vapour runs in a continuous fashion, before it reaches the next part: the condenser or 'serpentine' (resembling a coiled copper snake, used to turn alcohol vapour back into a liquid). Above this sits the third part: a wine vat, part warmed by the residual heat from the condenser, which allows the wine to start the distillation process at the optimum temperature.

These stills are quite spectacular: something of a steampunk marvel, they resemble the famous Victorian train, Stephenson's Rocket, with the open boiler blazing away, often fuelled by disused wooden stakes from the vineyard. The stills are made small enough to fit onto the back of a trailer, which is then towed around the region to the domains and growers who don't own a still themselves and require the services of a distiller-on-the-move. This portability means that even the smallest vine

← *Many Armagnac stills are wood-fired in the traditional manner.*

growers and wine makers can make Armagnac each year, even if only a handful of casks are produced. Armagnac only needs to be distilled once to obtain a very flavoursome and complex spirit at around 52% ABV. Cognac needs to be distilled twice to reach the same alcohol strength.

Some producers such as Samalens, founded in 1882 in the Bas-Armagnac region, use both the traditional continuous column still type and the double-distilled copper alembic stills used to produce Cognac. The two different distillate styles can then be blended or kept separate. This allows the distiller a broader spectrum of flavour, which gives Armagnac an even greater depth of character to that of Cognac.

With nearly 800 Armagnac producers and traders, it's easy enough to pop in and sample what the region has to offer.

THE
ARMAGNAC REGION

and its Grape Varieties

In 1936, the 'Decree of Armagnac' set out an AOC protection determining where grapes can be grown within Armagnac. These three sub regions are similar to Cognac's *crus*, though Armagnac's distinctions are arguably more down to the personality of the spirit produced, rather than the quality of production or spirit desirability.

THE THREE ARMAGNAC REGIONS

BAS ARMAGNAC

Covers more than half of the production of Armagnac, with its spirits highly prized as the most elegant examples.

ARMAGNAC-TÉNARÈZE

Built on more chalky soil and famed for its earthy, complex flavours.

HAUT-ARMAGNAC

Surrounds the other two regions and only accounts for a small percentage of Armagnac production.

MATURATION AND FLAVOUR

Like Cognac, Armagnac is matured exclusively in French oak barrels, primarily ones from the Monlezun forest. Over time the spirit develops its rich colour, with aromas of aged leather, dried fruit, spices and vanilla. Younger Armagnacs have similar flavours to Cognac – sweet vanilla and lightly honeyed notes – but older expressions can be truly amazing, developing a dry, weighty, complex character like aged Scotch whiskies.

In certain cases, particularly vintages from the late 1940s and 1950s, the mature spirit takes on a 'rancio' quality (a highly prized musty, savoury note, often found in very complex single malt whiskies matured in sherry casks). This pairs extremely well with robust Cuban cigars and other dominant flavours such as dark chocolate and coffee.

Armagnac is generally more affordable than Cognac, and whisky drinkers around the world are now seeking it out as a well-priced alternative to old Scotch and aged Japanese whisky.

K ey grapes for Armagnac production include the Baco grape (introduced in 1898 and accounting for 35 per cent of all production) and the highly popular Ugni Blanc (around 55 per cent). Folle Blanche (5 per cent) and Colombard (5 per cent) varieties are also used to give the briefly fermented wines different characteristics before they are distilled.

Baco is favoured for its robust qualities and it tends to age extremely well, while Folle Blanche is nicknamed the 'ballet dancer' for its temperamental traits during growth and the floral character it gives the finished Armagnac.

The Bureau National Interprofessionnel de l'Armagnac (BNIA), which controls the spirit's production and preservation, outlines ten specific grapes which can be used in Armagnac. This includes some rare varieties, such as Plant de Graisse, which are being brought back from the past as 'ghost varieties'. These are used in minute quantities to give the spirit an even wider range of characteristics.

The distillation of wines produced from these grapes traditionally happens in early November and, by law, must finish by no later than the end of March, so as not to use wine that has spoilt. Distillation may happen after these dates but the result can only be called 'brandy', not Armagnac.

CALVADOS

Calvados is the slightly left-field spirit in our *ménage à trois* of fine French brandy. Where Cognac and Armagnac are both straightforwardly grape-based, here we have a brandy that uses apples and pears to produce the base spirit, giving it a different style and flavour from our previous pair.

The Region

Calvados is located in Normandy in the northwest of France, where neither the temperature nor the soil quality are ideal for grape growing. But it is perfect for orchard fruits, and thus a spirit derived from these fruits.

Cider, made from the fermented juice of apples, has been produced since the 7th century in Normandy. Today, around 230 different varieties of apples and 140 of pear are called upon to make cider and perry, which can then be distilled into Calvados. Legally, Calvados must be aged in oak for no less than two years.

Styles

There are three *Appellations d'Origine Controlée* (AOC) in which Calvados can be made.

CALVADOS

Covers a vast area of lower Normandy, stretching into the neighbouring départements of Eure, Seine-Maritime, Mayenne, Sarthe and Oise. Produced using a column still, the Calvados AOC represents around 70 per cent of total Calvados production.

CALVADOS PAYS D'AUGE

East of the main Calvados region, with some areas on the borders of Orne and Eure, Calvados Pays d'Auge AOC is produced by double distillation in a traditional alembic pot still. A maximum of 30 per cent of the spirit can be from pears.

CALVADOS DOMFRONTAIS AOC

This region is famed for pears and, of the Calvados produced here, at least 30 per cent of every bottle must made from perry pears. Distillation happens in a column still, and it must be aged for a minimum of three years in oak.

> ↗ *Apple varieties ready for making into Calvados.*
>
> ← *Like Armagnac, Calvados has evolved from highly rustic processes.*

Ages

Calvados is matured – and labelled – as follows:

FINE, TROIS ÉTOILES OR TROIS POMMES

Minimum of two years in oak.

RÉSERVE OR VIEUX

Minimum of three years in oak.

VO, VSOP OR VIEILLE RESERVE

Minimum of four years in oak.

HORS D'AGE, XO, TRÈS VIEILLE RÉSERVE, TRÈS VIEUX, EXTRA OR NAPOLÉON

Minimum of six years in oak.

PRODUCTION FERMIÈRE

You might also see this on a bottle, denoting a brandy that has been exclusively farm-made, from harvest to bottling.

MARC: THE FRENCH GRAPPA

Marc is made from the leftover pomace (skins and pips) from a grape harvest. Rarely seen outside of France, it is also popular in the Burgundy, Champagne and Alsace regions, where the leftovers from the harvest of Pinot Noir, Chardonnay and Gewürztraminer wines are distilled and occasionally aged. The result resembles a fresh, grappa-like brandy, with the grape variety heavily influencing the flavour profile.

Enjoying

FRENCH BRANDY

You'll have seen people in bars swilling Cognac around in a classic brandy balloon glass or heating the vessel up with a candle to 'release the aroma'. This is indeed one method of enjoying good Cognac – but not the one we think is best.

Really great brandy deserves the same respect as any other expensive, rarefied aged spirit. Pour a measure into a fluted nosing glass, sit back and enjoy. This is true for any good Cognac, Armagnac or Calvados.

Brandies at the more accessible end of the market, VS and VSOP in particular, are often found in cocktails. Classics include the Side Car, Brandy Alexander and of course the Champagne Cocktail, where Champagne and Cognac are mixed with sugar and bitters. The Sazerac is a Cognac classic, though it sometimes calls for rye whisky instead.

Blanche Armagnac is designed for mixing and works wonders in a stirred down drink – as we shall see.

Joel & Neil's Perfect Serve

BLANCHE ARMAGNAC
MARTINI

Devilishly simple, this cocktail is all about celebrating the beautiful freshness found in a blanche-style Armagnac, which is bottled straight from the still at around 50% ABV. Older oak-aged Armagnacs make perfect contemplative sippers (as well as a great Old Fashioned), but Gascony's new kid on the block is most definitely turning a few heads in the cocktail market.

* **TWO PARTS BLANCHE ARMAGNAC**
* **ONE PART DRY VERMOUTH**
* **LEMON PEEL, TO GARNISH**

Add the Blanche Armagnac and vermouth to a mixing glass with plenty of ice. Stir for 45 seconds and strain into a chilled Martini glass. Zest a slice of lemon peel over the surface then drop the peel into the glass.

HOW TO MAKE

L E M O N   P E E L

BLANCHE
ARMAGNAC

DRY
VERMOUTH

10

ESSENTIAL FRENCH BRANDIES *TO TRY*

With a world of innovative new brands stepping up alongside the classics (which should never be discounted) and a delicious wave of new cocktails and serves, the curious spirits connoisseur in search of a spot of joie de vivre would do very well to look to Cognac, Armagnac and Calvados.

BEST IN GLASS «

» **Chateau de Lacquy 12 Years Old Armagnac**
40% | Lacquy, France
Gilles de Boisséson is the tenth generation of the same family to steer the spirit production at the 22-hectare Château Lacquy in Bas-Armagnac. Copper stills built in 1939 are still in use today, and the slow distillation process produces just two barrels a day of eau-de-vie. This 12-year-old expression carries gala melon and pear drops on the nose, with some oak aged Chardonnay notes, which give it real depth. The finish has light cinnamon and apple doughnut notes, with just a wisp of leather.

KEY

WOODY	SMOKY
NUTTY	GREEN FRUIT
FLORAL	RED FRUIT
MINERAL	HERBAL
SWEETNESS	SPICY
FATTY	CITRUS
CEREAL	VEGETAL

» Maison Ferrand 10 Generations Cognac
46% | Cognac, France
A Grande Champagne Cognac created to honour ten generations behind the Ferrand house. Made exclusively from the Ugni Blanc grape, a portion of which is matured in casks that previously held Sauternes wine, it delivers gingerbread spices and fresh pineapple and guava.

» Courvoisier XO Cognac
40% | Jarnac, France
From one of the most renowned houses of the region, this XO is a selection of eaux-de-vie matured from 11 to 25 years, and it gives a fresh, floral bouquet on the nose. Much like a good, boozy fruit cake, there's plenty of sultanas, raisins and orange rind on the palate, with a long, liquorice finish.

» H By Hine Cognac
40% | Jarnac, France
Drawing on 'Fine Champagne' grapes, that is grapes from both the Grande and Petite Champagne regions, this has a balance of polished wood, roasted almonds and toasted coffee beans. The palate is balanced with allspice, black cherry and creamy caramel. The finish is dry, medium in length and hints towards red apples.

» Frapin Cigar Blend XO Cognac
40% | Segonzac, France
Frapin makes a variety of Cognacs from grapes grown in its own vineyards and within the shadow of its chateau, Fontpinot, making it unique in the Grande Champagne region. Its Cigar Blend XO starts with hints of clear apple juice, but develops into cinnamon and oak spices, with enough delicate notes to let the fruit sing.

» Marc Darroze 30 Years Old Armagnac
50% | Roquefort, France
Darroze can rightfully be called one of the true pioneers of Armagnac, partly as the company has helped to make the spirit much more accessible outside of France. Its 30 year old is an explosion of dark cherries and marzipan, with a heavy woody influence and liquorice spiciness on the palate.

» Delamain Pale & Dry XO Cognac
42% | Jarnac, France
Delamain is a house that plays on the lighter side of Cognac. It shows off the more floral and fruity side of the Grande Champagne region, where oak gently kisses the spirit and no sugar or colouring is added. The Pale & Dry XO has fresh figs and peach melba notes, and the finish is nuanced and elegant.

» Casterède 1984 Armagnac
40% | Mauléon-d'Armagnac, France
Casterède is one of the world's oldest Armagnac houses and is still proudly family owned. There are some sensational younger spirits, notably the 10-year-old VSOP, but this 1984 vintage is exceptional. An explosion of grapes, nuts and apricots gives this excellent spirit real body and texture. A truly great year.

» Dupont Calvados Hors D'Age
42% | Victot-Pontfol, France
It seems unfair that Calvados is France's lesser-known brandy, after the more famous Cognac and Armagnac. But any sense of injustice is firmly swatted away when trying this Hors D'Age from the masterful Dupont family. Aged in oak for a minimum of six years – 25 per cent from new oak casks – this has zesty notes and banana bread, jasmine flowers, spice and intense apple on the palate.

» Avallen Calvados
40% | Manche, France
An independent Calvados company that srtives to be sustainable. Part of the '1% for the Planet' scheme, it donates a percentage of its turnover to organisations that help protect the bees that pollinate the apple and pear trees of the region. Aged in French oak barrels for at least two years, it gives notes of honey, crisp apples and lavender.

WORLD BRANDY

a fruitful, flavoursome affair

WORLD BRANDY

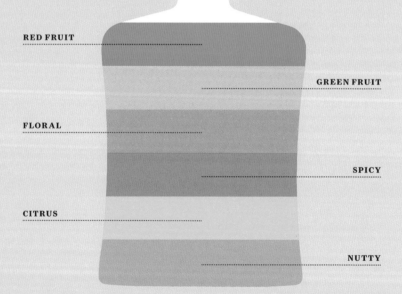

FLAVOUR & AROMA

RED FRUIT

GREEN FRUIT

FLORAL

SPICY

CITRUS

NUTTY

Brandy represents the very essence of a *national spirit*, born of ingenuity, necessity – and, yes, a desire for alcohol. It has infiltrated pretty much every corner of the earth over the last 500 years, fusing idiosyncratic flavours with traditional production methods.

What makes it such a successful, widely loved category is that it can basically be made anywhere. Grapes are grown everywhere from Europe to South Africa, the Middle East and across the US, and brandy gives wine makers a way to protect their investment: if they can't sell their wines due to poor harvest or other challenges, the grapes won't go to waste, with the distillate 'brandies' finding favour outside of the circles of traditional wine drinkers. Similarly, the waste by-products of wine making have a purpose, with the discarded skins and pips – more commonly known as the pomace or marc – all finding their way into highly palatable brandies.

Growers of other fruits have got in on the game too. Fruit brandy or, to give the category its proper title, eau-de-vie, can be made from almost any variety of fruit as the naturally high fructose content means plenty of highly fermentable sugars to brew and distil. Europe has a strong history of orchard fruit eaux-de-vie using plums, apples, pears, apricots and cherries, with many of these spirits becoming ingrained in the distilling country's culture. Over the following chapter, we'll visit some of the most exciting of these, from pisco to pálinka, and discover a few of the fine producers who have mastered the art of turning fruit into liquid gold.

SPANISH GRAPE
BRANDY

A Taste of Andalusian Gold

Jerez de la Frontera, in Spain's Andalusia region, is home to the country's finest Sherry houses, from Gonzalez Byass and Lustau to Pedro Domecq and Williams & Humbert, whose Sherries have – excuse the pun – fortified the palates of many a drinks enthusiast. Single malt lovers too will be familiar with Jerez, as it is here that the world's most prized cooperages can be found making casks for a handful of the most prestigious players in Scotch. But Jerez isn't only about Sherry and single malt. It produces a plethora of wonderful brandy too.

Brandy de Jerez can trace its roots back to the late 1500s, although it is likely that distillation in the region dates way back beyond this. The brandies used to be shipped internationally under the moniker of Coñac Fundador, a term which was only dropped in the 1970s. Brandy de Jerez can utilize grapes grown from anywhere in Spain, with the most popular varieties being the

↑ *Casks of Brandy de Jerez maturing peacefully.*

↗ *González Byass distillery not only produces great Sherry, but brandy too.*

Airén and the Palomino, which is widely used in the production of Sherry.

Brandy de Jerez is usually distilled once, either in traditionally shaped wood fired pot stills (called *alquitaras*) or column stills, with different cut points (see page 13) and styles of spirit blended to create the final brandy recipe. The maturation must occur within Jerez, in American oak casks which have previously held different Sherries. The Sherry in question has a huge effect on the resulting brandy: those which held drier styles such as Oloroso or Palo Cortado impart nutty, aromatic qualities to the maturing brandy, whereas casks formerly filled with Pedro Ximénez give a huge sweetness, alongside dried fruit notes.

One other weapon in the Jerez distiller's arsenal is what's known as the solera system, widely used in Sherry blending but also in spirits too. A batch of brandy is put in a vat before being bottled, with the oldest casks being periodically added to the vat to give a greater complexity. The system ensures a consistent complexity across different batches. When bottled, these brandies are classified into three offerings: Solera is aged on average for six months; Solera Reserva is aged for a minimum of one year; and Solera Gran Reserva is aged for a minimum of three years.

ENJOYING BRANDY DE JEREZ

There are some subtle similarities, particularly an earthiness, to a youthful Armagnac. Unsurprisingly there are also a plethora of Sherry-driven flavours, which make this brandy an absolute treat to the senses. Younger examples are drier in style, with lighter citrus and floral notes, whereas an older Gran Reserva is complex and rich with dark chocolate, tobacco, dried fruit and spice notes. Especially interesting are the bottlings that list the main cask finish used in the maturation: an intensely rich Pedro Ximénez cask, for example, brings a full-on Christmas-cake-in-a-glass note to the brandy.

GRAPPA

The Italian Maestro

Travel anywhere across Italy and you'll find an infectious obsession with all things home grown. From food to fashion and Ferrari, the Italians pour their heart and soul into the things they love. And spirits are no exception. To the north of the country, you'll find the heartland of grappa, a pomace brandy made from grape seeds and skins. It's undoubtedly the oldest spirit produced in Italy, with a history dating back to the 14th century.

Grappa's rustic history means that it hasn't been as widely appreciated as it should be. Once dismissed as a harsh, warming spirit consumed by farmers in the colder months, quality grappas from long established producers, and often based around the specific flavours of grape varietals, are now finding favour among spirits connoisseurs globally.

GRAPPA PRODUCTION AND GRAPE VARIETIES

Making grappa is a tricky business – and not one which yields much spirit, or profit. The by-products used – the stems, seeds and skins of grapes, known as the pomace – are tough to work with and roughly 100kg of pomace is needed to produce just five litres of grappa.

Of the grape varieties used, more aromatic styles such as Gewürztraminer, Moscato and Sauvignon Blanc are popular with distillers, bringing a lighter, floral and exceptionally fruity element to the finished spirit. Some distillers favour heavier styles of varietal, including Merlot and the powerful Barolo, which bring a bolder, darker and altogether richer, drier fruitiness, with bittersweet jam notes and hints of earthiness and spice. Pomace comes in three types, which impact the overall style of the spirit: unfermented white wine pomace, partly fermented rosé pomace and finally a fully fermented red wine pomace.

Across the industry, a more modern style of column distillation is favoured for its

Aged grappas can fall into three styles. *Invecchiata* has a cask maturation of no fewer than 12 months. The older, more wood-driven style of *riserva* needs to be matured in casks for no less than 18 months. Finally, *stravecchia* needs to be aged for over two years (and usually well beyond) and comes from the most highly prized vines. (See our pick from Nardini on page 171, which is aged for seven years.)

ENJOYING GRAPPA

Given the diversity of grape varietals and the myriad wood styles used in cask matured grappas, there is a vast range of flavours to be found in grappa: fresh, slightly sweet ripe fruit, vivid citrus notes, tart, green fruit notes, woody spice and toasted, nutty elements. Traditionally, it is enjoyed neat, at room temperature, in a small, specifically designed glass which helps to highlight the aromatic fruitiness or bolder spiciness. One tradition of Italian cafés is a Caffè Coretto, in which the spirit is combined with freshly brewed espresso coffee to bring out even more complexity on the palate. Grappa is also finding plenty of favour with international bartenders as an alternative in gin-based cocktails, where the more botanical freshness of young, unaged grappas or the *aromatizzata* styles bring something really rather exciting to the world of cocktails.

simplicity and efficiency, but more craft-oriented distillers prefer hybrid stills, with both pot and column elements, which keep more of the distinct flavours from grape varieties. Once distilled, the clear spirit is collected at around 86% ABV, then diluted with demineralized water and bottled at a more palatable strength.

Grappa is bottled both unaged and after maturation in a variety of wood types, each one imparting another unique character to the spirit. The unaged style, known in Italy as *giovane*, is often rested in large stainless steel vessels for around a year, which helps to marry some of the more volatile elements, bringing an overall harmony to the finished product.

When aged, grappa takes on an extremely broad spectrum of new flavours and aromas. Distillers and blenders aren't limited to using oak, and can call upon the likes of chestnut, cherry and mulberry casks, to bring additional fruitiness, alongside drier, spicy tannins and nutty notes. The major challenge is balance: a great grappa needs the grape varietal to sing in perfect harmony alongside the additional – often very dominant – flavours from the cask type. Not at all easy to achieve.

↑ *Preparing the pomace for grappa production by hand.*

FRUIT BRANDIES

From the Garden of England to the Valleys of Eastern Europe

The ubiquity of the humble grape combined with the dogged determination with which distillers extract every drop of flavour from them makes for some incredible spirits. So too with other fruits, particularly those across western and eastern Europe.

One of Germany, Austria and Switzerland's most popular fruit-based spirits is Kirschwasser, distilled from fermented Morello cherry pulp. Ripe cherries are full of sweet juice, giving the distiller an excellent base from which to work. Kirschwasser has an intense, very clean, almost tart fruitiness to it, with the underlying cherry note accompanied by a distinct almond-like nuttiness. This comes from the fermentation process, as every bit of the cherry (including the stones) is used.

Because cherry trees grow in abundance across Germany (especially around the Rhine and Alsace) and Switzerland – where there are around 800 varieties of cherry recorded – the art of Kirsch distilling

is taken very seriously. Some distillers release theirs as fresh as possible; others take the time to age the spirit in either stainless steel or glass – sometimes for up to four years to tame the bite of the young distillate. The most premium Kirschwassers are *jahrgangskirsch*, from a specific

↑ *Kirsch production is seen as an exacting science by its distillers.*

vintage and single varietal cherry harvest where the fruit has been deemed absolutely exceptional. These bottlings, which have an incredibly complex palate and intensely aromatic, fruity nose, are few and far between – so make sure to grab one if you see it.

Eastern Europe has a raging thirst for fruit-derived brandies. Hungary has pálinka (a legally protected fruit-spirit category, recognized by the EU since 2004) while slivovitz, a hugely popular damson plum-based brandy, is distilled across Bosnia, Poland, Slovakia and Ukraine. Both are produced by fermenting the pulp and stones of the fruit (for pálinka, these must be grown in Hungary and must come from a concentrate) with yeast and then distilling in small pot stills. In Bulgaria, Croatia, Serbia and Macedonia you'll come across rakija, another fruit-based brandy, bottled at a minimum of 37.5% ABV and often aged in casks.

ENGLAND'S RENAISSANCE

Kent in the southeast of England has historically been known as the Garden of England, thanks to the abundance of fruit orchards. While various laws once made it tricky for new distillers, today there is a growing band of artisans who have begun to explore heritage varieties of fruit not used in distillation for centuries. Quince, pears, apples, medlars, mulberries and gooseberries are all being used to create imaginative eaux-de-vies which explode with freshness, and are also undergoing innovative ageing in oak and chestnut casks.

In the southwest, there's a welcome renaissance of England's apple brandy tradition, with distillers such as Julian Temperley and Tim Stoddart exploring some of the hundreds of apple varieties for which the region is famed.

MEET THE MAKER

}

Barney Wilczak

FOUNDER, CAPREOLUS DISTILLERY

Tell us a little bit about the concept of Capreolus and how you got into distilling fruit eau-de-vie.

Distilling eau-de-vie really evolved from a love of plants and a former life as a photojournalist working in conservation. Teaching myself through translating texts from the masters of fruit distilling, I developed my own way of working that stepped away from the traditional drivers of yield to a purely qualitative approach. I became fascinated by the way in which drawing these perfumes from our local fruits revealed so much not only about the fruit but, through sheer compression, the parent plants and our maritime climate.

What's the biggest challenge you face on a day-to-day basis?

Harvest is a four-month process, with wild fermentations taking up to 19 weeks. The season takes up to eight and a half months from start to finish, and there are the logistical challenges of working to ripeness, not a calendar. The days are long and contain a good degree of physicality. However, there is a great deal of excitement for the potential of quality fruit, and it is really the mundane daily issues of space and finding enough hours in the day that are the real challenges!

What's the secret behind creating a great eau-de-vie and what do you look for in every Capreolus release?

It sounds trite, but respect. We have such complexity in the fruits that we work with. Long ago, I came to the acceptance that I couldn't create anything more complex than nature. Therefore, it is working with care and precision; timing for harvest, hand grading every single berry, quince or apple, long fermentations, distilling at the right point, never recycling the negative parts of the spirit and looking for vitality over yield. It means that we keep less than half of the amount (up to 45kg fruit/litre) that most fruit distillers do but we have something that is evocative of the place where we live. Stylistically, I look for a balance between expansive perfume, concentration and great delicacy.

How do you drink eau-de-vie at home?

Typically as a digestif at room temperature: it's the best way to experience aroma, flavour and texture. However, we follow some of the chefs with whom we work, and also add a few drops as pure essence to ice cream, tarte tatin or sauces!

Any great cocktails you have come across, which have changed your perception of how the fruit brandy category is evolving?

Coming from this digestif background, I have been fascinated to see how bartenders are able to use bitters-like amounts that still dominate with their perfume. Perhaps the most famous example has been the Pastel by Remy Savage and the team at A Bar with Shapes for a Name [an award-winning experimental London cocktail joint] that sees just 2.5ml of our raspberry eau-de-vie singing over the top of a base of rhubarb, lime and vodka – incredibly delicious!

Finally, sum up Capreolus in just three words.

Perfume. Delicacy. Obsession.

AMERICAN BRANDY & APPLEJACK

The Next Flavoursome Frontier?

The US may be known for its world class bourbon and rye whiskey, but it also has a long heritage of fruit distillation, including Applejack, an apple-based brandy which can trace its roots back to 1698. Thought originally to be the product of freeze distillation, where an apple cider has the water separated or 'jacked' from the alcohol by freezing it, it has a sharp, fresh, orchard fruit aroma and palate. The Laird's brand has been in existence since 1780, surviving Prohibition and the spirit's decline in popularity. However, Applejack appears to be on the rise once again, with a number of smaller craft operations opening up which look set to revive one of the USA's fallen spirits.

↓ *A small cooperage producing casks to store applejack.*

PISCO

The Spirited Star of South America

Those searching for a taste of South America have a few superb options from which to choose on the global back bar. If you're a rum fanatic, you'll likely have come across Brazilian cachaça (see page 57) perhaps enjoyed in the form of the Caipirinha.

From Argentina, you'll find *aguardiente* – a grape-based spirit – and hesperidina, an orange-based bitter aperitif often enjoyed with tonic, and one of the first drinks brands to receive protected status in the country. But dearest to our hearts is pisco: a sweet

spirit distilled from grapes, the origins of which are hotly contested between the neighbouring countries of Chile and Peru.

Pisco was developed in the 16th century when Spanish settlers set up vineyards and, from the by-products of the wine making process, began making a Peruvian version of the Spanish pomace brandy grappa. As the popularity of this sweet spirit grew, both the Peruvian and Chilean people claimed ownership over it. There are now strictly controlled areas for pisco production in both countries. Chilean pisco is often bottled at around 30% ABV, lower than its Peruvian rival, and each country strictly limits the grape varieties which can be used. Currently there are eight varietals sanctioned in Peru: Quebranta, Negra Criolla, Uvina and Mollar are non-aromatic, and Moscatel, Torontel, Italia and Albilla are aromatic, with the lion's share of Peruvian pisco being made from Quebranta. Over in Chile, there are five varietals: the aromatic Moscatel de Alejandría, Moscatel Rosada and Torontel, as well as non-aromatic Pedro Ximénez and Moscatel de Austria.

As with Cognac and grappa, the grape variety is hugely important when it comes to the style and flavour of different piscos and, like wine, these grapes can be blended (known as *acholado* pisco) to give each brand its own individual profile.

The distillation of pisco in each country differs too. Peruvian pisco is only distilled once in small alembic pot stills and bottled undiluted, with no water permitted. The same applies in Chile but the rectifying column still can also

be used in conjunction with the alembic. The spirit can also be diluted to a bottling strength. One fascinating aspect of pisco production is the almost complete lack of ageing. In Peru, the regulations do permit wood ageing, which is not the case in Chile, although there are very few examples of wood-aged Peruvian pisco available.

ENJOYING PISCO

Pisco has a sweet, fruity, sometimes drier earthy note, but the aromatic grape varieties – particularly Albilla and Italia – bring in some superb orchard fruit and freshly cut flower notes, full of fragrant green apple and elderflower character. *Puro* piscos are made from a single variety of grape and, like Italian grappa, highlight the incredibly multifaceted nature of this eloquent spirit.

No matter where your pisco comes from, you'll want to enjoy a Pisco Sour as the first port of call. This truly wondrous cocktail, which brings together pisco, fresh lime juice, sugar syrup, egg white and Angostura bitters, was first conceived in Lima back in the 1910s. The spirit became hugely popular in San Francisco during the Californian Gold Rush, when Peruvians arrived in the city to mine, and was enjoyed in a punch and as a neat shot. San Franciscans have yet to tire of the cocktail, and today the USA remains the biggest importer of pisco.

MEET
THE
MAKER

Catalina Bentz

FOUNDER, CATAN PISCO

Tell us what you do, Catalina.
I'm the founder of Catan Pisco, the USA's first pisco brand, and I am humbled to be the first Chilean woman founder of a pisco company! I was born in Santiago, Chile, with an entrepreneurial spirit.

What's the biggest challenge you face on a day-to-day basis?
The biggest challenge I face is getting American bars to take a leap of faith in placing Catan Pisco on their menus. I get a lot of push back because 'no one knows what it is' but this is exactly why we need to support this spirit. A lot of managers are hesitant to try my pisco, as they have had bad experiences in the past with other not-so-premium pisco brands. I've endeavoured to create the most well balanced pisco in our market and I am so proud to have had this validated after entering my first spirits competition in San Diego, where it took home a Double Gold and, out of 400 different spirits entries, was voted Best in Show.

What's the secret to creating a great pisco recipe?
The secret is staying true to my discriminatory palate. I love sipping on a good whisky, and I knew I wanted to create a sip-worthy pisco. Many different batches were flown out to me from my distillery partners in Chile but nothing was good enough. I had to fly out there and be fully transparent with my vision of Catan's profile.

After 18 months we finally got it right and for the first time in Chilean pisco history, my recipe consisted of 100 per cent Pedro Ximénez grape. The second I tasted this varietal I knew my baby was officially born!

How do you drink your pisco at home?
I love to sip on it, naturally, but lately I've been obsessed with Pisco-tinis: Catan with vermouth (either a Spanish *blanco* or *rojo*) just blows my mind. Grapes dancing with other grapes, creating fireworks every time on my palate. With a grape garnish, it's the perfect cocktail.

Are there any great cocktails you have come across, which have changed your perception of pisco's versatility?
I am surprised every day at how versatile pisco is, from pisco Palomas to Pisco with Averna [Sicilian amaro: a bitter, spicy fortified wine, in the same vein as a vermouth]. Simply switching pisco into any boring vodka cocktail just upscales the drinking experience.

Finally, sum up Catan in just three words.
Balanced. Sexy. Versatile.

Joel & Neil's Perfect Serve

PISCO SOUR

Nothing makes us feel quite as right with the world as a well-made Pisco Sour on a hot summer's day. Sure, there are simpler drinks to make, but combine a fresh, aromatic pisco, the bite of lime, sweetness and frothy egg white, and it's a pretty good value way to be transported to a buzzing bar in the streets of Lima or Santiago.

* TWO PARTS PISCO (CAMPO DE ENCANTO OR CATAN ARE IDEAL)
* ONE PART FRESHLY SQUEEZED LIME JUICE
* HALF PART SUGAR SYRUP
* ONE FRESH EGG WHITE (OR ONE PART AQUAFABA FOR A VEGAN OPTION)
* A FEW DROPS OF ANGOSTURA BITTERS

Add all the ingredients (except the bitters) to a shaker with ice. Shake vigorously for 20–30 seconds and strain into a rocks glass over more ice. To finish, add a few drops of Angostura bitters atop the foamy head.

HOW TO MAKE

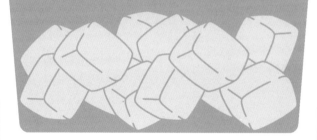

BITTERS

BITTERS

EGG WHITE

SUGAR SYRUP

LIME JUICE

PISCO

10

ESSENTIAL WORLD BRANDIES *TO TRY*

With the sheer wealth of base ingredients to choose from, the world of brandy outside the French classics really knows no bounds. If you're feeling a little fruity, look no further.

BEST IN GLASS «

» Capreolus Quince Eau-de-Vie 2022

43% | Cotswolds, England

For Barney Wilczak, a former photojournalist turned craft distiller (see page 160) the idyllic surroundings of his childhood Cotswolds home prompted him to explore just how close he could get to capturing the freshness of heritage fruits in an eau-de-vie. After a decade of trying to master the art of slow, wild fermentation, he insists he's still learning – but we think he's nailed it. This quince-based spirit is wonderfully ripe, with crisp, aromatic apple notes, lemon zest and freshly cut roses.

KEY

● WOODY	● SMOKY
● NUTTY	● GREEN FRUIT
● FLORAL	● RED FRUIT
● MINERAL	● HERBAL
● SWEETNESS	● SPICY
● FATTY	● CITRUS
● CEREAL	● VEGETAL

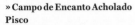

» Campo de Encanto Acholado Pisco

40.5% | Peru (via San Francisco)
Established by three San Franciscan spirits enthusiasts, this is an *acholado*-style pisco – a blend of aromatic and non-aromatic grapes, including Quebranta, Torontel, Moscotel and the wonderfully floral Italia variety, all of which slowly mingle over a year's resting.

» Catan Pisco Reserve

40% | Chile via the USA
Catalina Bentz is the first female founder of a Chilean pisco brand, and determined to open up to a new audience (see page 166). Catan is a single varietal pisco using organic, Fairtrade-certified Pedro Ximénez grapes from near the Andes. Think fresh peaches, ripe tangerines and melon, alongside orange blossom and magnolia floral notes.

» Vecchia Romagna Etichetta Nera Brandy

38% | Bologna, Italy
Settled in Bologna, by way of Napoleonic France, Vecchia Romagna's Etichetta Nera is distilled using Ugni Blanc. It combines continuous and alembic distillation before ageing in wine barriques and smaller casks. Tropical fruits sit with rich vanilla and woody, oak-driven spices.

» Metaxa Private Reserve

40% | Athens/Samos, Greece
Metaxa has a complex makeup. It brings together Muscat wines from Samos, grape-based distillates, and a 'tincture' blend of fine herbs and Mediterranean botanicals. A final cask ageing, and the result is a remarkable journey on the palate. The Private Reserve is rich, spicy, unctuous and sweet, with chocolate notes and floral overtones.

» Burnt Faith Small Batch Brandy

40% | London, England
Burnt Faith sounds like a racing dog but that's where similarities with its local area, Walthamstow, end. The distillery is the city's first dedicated to brandy, and takes Cognac traditions to a new level. Using four grape varieties with a range of cask types, it has created a genuine thoroughbred.

» Reisetbauer Kirsch

41.5% | Linz-Land, Austria
This is a fantastic Kirsch. The technologically advanced distillery was recently revitalized with minute temperature controls giving a precision like no other. More than 3.5kg of ripe cherries are used in each bottle, resulting in a bright, crisp yet wonderfully soft fruity aroma with an almond and chocolate-led palate.

» St George Pear Brandy

40% | California, USA
The OG craft distillery in the USA. St George has turned its hand to gin, single malt and many an experimental spirit; it even distilled a Christmas tree and made it taste great. This brandy uses 30lb (13.5kg) of Bartlett pears (or Williams pears) per bottle. It's fermented for 10 days and distilled once to capture the closest fruit flavours possible. Wonderfully rich but bright and fresh.

» Nardini Riserva 7-Year-Old Grappa

45% | Bassano del Grappa, Italy
The Nardini name is one of the most significant in the grappa world. The distillery dates back to 1779, making it the oldest producer by some margin. This seven-year-old riserva manages to bring all the classic fresh, bright, aromatic fruit notes alongside a perfectly well-rounded, oak-driven softness. A true delight from the masters of the spirit.

» Lepanto Solera Gran Reserva Brandy

40% | Jerez, Spain
This outstanding brandy, produced by legendary Sherry company Gonzalez Byass, is aged for 12 years in a solera vat, instilling marvellous depth, before it is transferred into deliciously rich and spicy Pedro Ximénez sherry casks for a final three years maturation. Here it takes on a heavenly complexity, alongside woody spice, tobacco notes and intense dried fruit.

VODKA

clarity,
balance...
and taste

VODKA

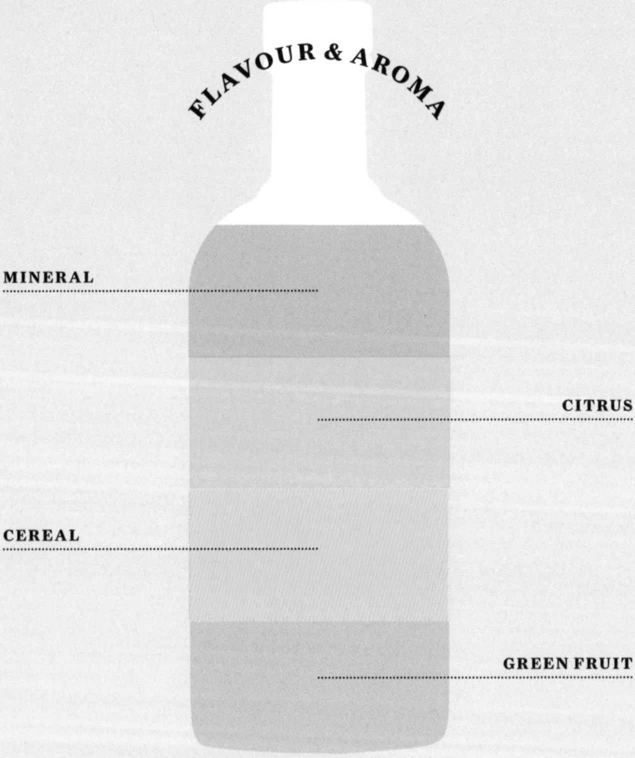

FLAVOUR & AROMA

MINERAL

CITRUS

CEREAL

GREEN FRUIT

Vodka is the purest of spirits. Its neutrality and thus versatility has made it ubiquitous around the globe. It's enjoyed as a simple plus one to cola, soda and lime, or ginger ale, and also as the foundation of a spicy Mule or the firepower in Mr Bond's signature Martini. Today, it's more often sipped neat over ice or gulped chilled as a shot. Though vodka may have recently lost the battle with gin as the clear spirit du jour, it certainly hasn't tapped out yet.

O ver the past decade, vodka has suffered from a chorus of unwarranted criticism. It's been deemed boring, flavourless and bland; dismissed as a mere alcoholic booster to up the potency of an existing drink; sidelined in favour of brighter, trendier stars in the world of mixology.

These days are thankfully fading into the past, as a new generation of bartenders and connoisseurs looks to vodka's roots. The interest now lies in finely balanced spirit character, purity and flavour, all of which are fundamentally driven by the spirit's base ingredients.

Alongside this, some brands are transporting consumers back to the past (see Belvedere on page 187) to a world where consistency, ubiquity and neutrality weren't the watchwords they are now in the global spirits industry.

Vodka's true power lies in the fact that, despite its Eastern European origins, it can be made anywhere, from any base ingredient (more on this later). It can be conveniently infused, flavoured or enhanced with other – often subtle – ingredients, ensuring that it has become, quite frankly, an essential spirit across the world.

PURITY

Vodka's Misinterpreted Descriptor

In its most basic form, vodka is nothing but a distilled spirit – pure and simple. In the past, this aspect came to quite rigidly define its quality and price point, and dictated how consumers valued it – the latter mostly driven by sneaky spirits marketeers, rather than the distillers themselves.

A fashion for distilling – and filtering – a vodka as many times as possible (occasionally through such nonsense as diamonds) gained vodka a reputation as a super-clean spirit that tasted of nothing and wouldn't leave you with a wild hangover the day after. For the kind of drinker who didn't really like the taste of alcohol, this was utter genius. For the spirits connoisseur, this marketing ploy had the opposite effect. They saw expensive premium vodkas as bland and characterless, as a certain amount of spirit impurity brings inherent mouthfeel and thus – surprise surprise – perceptible flavour. Though 'purity' was marketed as a positive, in practice the more a spirit is distilled, the more it is rectified to remove complex chemical compounds, oils and congeners – and the more its natural flavour and personality is stripped away.

In response, the smarter new players who came to define the new golden age of vodka over two decades ago – Cîroc, Grey Goose, Absolut – reimagined purity as something else: harmony in the overall balance of their respective spirits.

They sought high quality base ingredients, such as grapes once destined for Cognac production; golden winter wheat, the character of which wasn't distilled away to nothing; potatoes, to give a sweet, creamy mouthfeel and structure; and pure glacial mineral water, which was used to bring down the strength of the spirit, but also gave body and texture. This effectively created a whole new category of vodka. Brands were still able to sell expensive products and even offer ultra-premium editions, previously not seen in the simple world of vodka, but also bring much more flavour and personality to the table.

VODKA'S

Murky Past

Now a bastion of purity, the origins of vodka are considerably cloudier. It has fuelled much mythology, been the centrepiece of political conflict and served to loosen tongues in countless espionage chronicles the world over. Today, the global vodka market is larger than any other spirit, with more than 680 million litres sold in the US alone each year, where annual sales top $7 billion.

It is unclear where the first vodkas were actually distilled. Russia and Poland both claim to have shaped the spirit in its current iteration – as do Ukraine and Finland where harsh weather conditions complicated the import of beer and wine as both liquids would freeze in transit because of their high water content. In the late 1970s, the Soviet Union and Poland waged a battle over the exclusive rights to label their brands with the word 'vodka', with both sides citing historical

texts that alluded to its origins. It is almost certain that the term 'vodka' can be traced back to the Slavic word *woda*, meaning water. Polish court documents reveal that almost as far back as 1405, the word had been used in reference to medicinal and pharmaceutical use of the spirit. In Russia, the description goes a step further with the term *khlebny vino* – 'bread wine' –

referring to the 'dilution with water' of a grain-based distilled spirit for medical purposes. There are also suggestions that the etymology of vodka is linked to the Slavic word 'to burn' – in Polish, *gorzalka* – perhaps referring to the exceedingly high temperatures required during the distillation process.

Primitive distillation of grain often led to a rough, impure spirit that was unpleasant to the nose, let alone the palate. To compensate, flavourings such as herbs were often added to make spirits more palatable as medicinal tinctures. More professional distilling production began in the early 15th century, which is when spirit began to be developed for consumption.

By the end of the 16th century, vodka had become a widely consumed beverage across Eastern Europe, with different grains used according to crop harvests. The Polish author Jakub Kazimierz Haur mentions rye as a key ingredient in vodka distillation in his 1693 book *A Treasury of Excellent Secrets about Landed Gentry's Economy* – the title referencing the fact that Polish nobility were given a production monopoly of the spirit. The high alcoholic strength of the early vodkas was considerably reduced by the addition of water and by the end of the century, some of the first vodkas brands such as Goldwasser (one of the first commercially available herb-infused spirits) and Żubrówka started to emerge.

Over in Tsarist Russia, vodka distillation and distribution had become a government regulated process, which provided huge levels of taxation revenue. The first 'Tsar's Kabak', a place where various alcoholic drinks (including vodka) could be bought and consumed, was opened in 1533. By the mid-18th century, state manufactured

↑ *Vodka has always been a sociable spirit!*

← *Vodka peddler, circa 1640.*

↓ *The interior of Tsar Nikolai II's vodka distillery, 1901.*

vodka was the drink of choice for citizens of all standing, with consumption growing enormously when the strict laws governing production were repealed and the spirit became affordable to rich and poor alike.

As demand grew, the quality of the spirit had to be refined and the purity levels increased, leading to the first breakthroughs in 'rectification', or filtration by re-distillation. By 1768, it was commonplace for the spirit to be distilled three times to increase strength and reduce impurities. In 1843, the national standard for vodka was established in Russia. Since the taxation laws on alcoholic drinks were based on their strength, 40% ABV was decided upon to simplify matters.

DISTILLING VODKA

The Origins of Flavour

While it is now commonplace for vodka brands to use a single grain type (such as rye, wheat, corn, sorghum or barley), originally a multitude of base ingredients were used. Potatoes and sugar beets produced a cheap fermentable mash, often seen as inferior to that distilled from more expensive wheat or rye crops. Ironically, today some of the best vodkas in the world are distilled using specific, highly prized varietals of potatoes. Molasses is also a popular base ingredient for more mainstream, high volume vodka brands due to its consistent alcohol yield and global availability.

The distillation of vodka follows similar procedures to that of rum or single malt whisky, using a traditional pot-still and/or column still.

The re-distillation and filtration process, as mentioned earlier, is where vodka gains its (perceived) purity.

Mainstream vodka brands are often re-distilled up to eight times, then filtered slowly through long columns of charcoal, quartz sand and even precious metals. This process removes a great deal of the flavour compounds. By contrast, some modern, premium brands such as Absolut, Ketel One and Belvedere seek to retain as much flavour from the base ingredients as possible by only distilling the spirit two or three times, or even just once.

Today, base ingredients extend far beyond root

Enjoying Vodka

vegetables and grains. The game changed considerably back in 2003, when winemaker Jean-Sébastien Robicquet created Cîroc vodka using grapes grown in the Cognac region of France. More grape varietal vodkas are now springing up and canny distillers are looking towards their own local produce including, of all things, milk, as popularized by Dorset's Black Cow Vodka and now Blacklion from the Cotswolds, which uses sheep's milk. Each base ingredient makes its mark in the finished spirit: from the subtle maltiness of wheat to the fresher sweetness of corn or a peppery spice from rye. Those prize potatoes (including Jersey Royals) bring a buttery soft note and grapes fruitiness.

Vodka has also been infused with additional flavours for centuries. Traditionally across Russia, landowners would bottle their own specific flavour of vodka, utilizing fruit and berries such as cherry, pear and blackberry, as well as more obscure flavourings including acorn, caraway seed, sage and dill. In Scandinavia, a host of flavoured vodkas are drunk in celebration of seasonal festivals, with Sweden boasting as many as 40 different varieties.

Because of its versatility, vodka has found itself the sidekick to almost every mixer under the sun. However, it is now finally creeping into the spotlight, and drinkers are exploring the flavoursome merits of the spirit either neat, or in simpler 'straight up' cocktails, which anchor their flavour around the spirit. We must say, a shot of perfectly clean, highly chilled vodka straight from the freezer, with its viscous, unctuous mouthfeel and the fire it builds in your belly, is an experience like no other. The Eastern European tradition (arguably still the best) is to consume vodka this way with a variety of sublimely flavoured foods such as delicate salty caviar; sweet, malted rye bread; pickles; and rich, spicy soups and stews such as borscht, bigos or goulash.

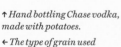

↑ *Hand bottling Chase vodka, made with potatoes.*

← *The type of grain used imparts a signature flavour characteristic into a quality vodka.*

Joel & Neil's Perfect Serve

St. CLEMENT'S

Who doesn't love a Cosmopolitan? The pink drink of neon nightclubs is a sure fire winner in our book. But if you've not got cranberry juice to hand – or fancy a sweeter, fresher, more zest-laden kick – then give this a whirl.

* ONE PART VODKA – WE RECOMMEND SOMETHING NEUTRAL, LIKE CONNIE GLAZE (SEE PAGE 186) OR BELVEDERE

* TWO PARTS FRESHLY SQUEEZED ORANGE JUICE

* ONE PART COINTREAU

* HALF PART FRESHLY SQUEEZED LEMON JUICE

Add all the ingredients to a shaker filled with ice and shake for 12–15 seconds. Strain into a coupe glass.

HOW TO MAKE

LEMON
JUICE

COINTREAU

ORANGE
JUICE

VODKA

MEET THE MAKER

}

Alex Christou

FOUNDER, EIGHT LANDS

Tell us what you do, Alex and a bit about yourself.
I am the founder of Eight Lands. In the early days this meant overseeing the construction of Glenrinnes Distillery in Scotland and working to develop our brand and, of course, our recipes. Today, we remain a small team and I continue to oversee all elements of the business. It is my job to guide the direction of the brand, make sure that our staff and suppliers are paid promptly, spend time with our international distribution partners, host VIP visits to Glenrinnes, and ensure that we never lose our focus on quality. I still sign-off every batch of Eight Lands vodka personally.

What's the biggest challenge you face on a day-to-day basis?
As a young brand, our biggest challenge is introducing Eight Lands to new audiences. We have total belief in the quality of our spirit but we recognise that reaching new customers, telling our story and giving them the chance to try our organic vodka can be tricky. We simply don't have the budgets of the big brands so it's important for us to look at unique assets – such as our Speyside-based distillery – and how these can help us build relationships with bartenders and spirits enthusiasts around the world.

What's the secret behind creating a great vodka recipe and what do you look for in Eight Lands products?
I believe that people too often overlook the main ingredient in vodka: water. We draw our water from a small spring located just behind our distillery (it's why we chose this site), which sits on our organic estate and therefore avoids the possible run-off of pesticides that many water sources are subject to. Our neighbours – some of the best-known single malt whiskies in the world – have done a brilliant job of explaining the importance of water in their products. We want to do the same with ours. I also think that people don't talk about 'cut points' enough in vodka. A lot of connoisseurs have heard about 'heads', 'tails' and 'hearts' in whisky production. The same stands for vodka. To get a great quality vodka, you need to focus on only bottling the best quality liquid.

How do you drink vodka at home?
I'm a Martini lover. That's always a go-to for me at home, preferably stirred and with a lemon twist and a splash of medium-dry vermouth.

However, I'm often reminded how good Eight Lands vodka is simply over ice or even out of the freezer, as I know a number of our customers enjoy it. As one friend put it: 'freeze, serve, enjoy'.

Any great cocktails you have come across, which have changed your perception of how vodka is evolving as a spirit?
I think vodka's versatility as a cocktail ingredient remains undimmed. Rather than choosing a vodka for your cocktail based on it being essentially anonymous, you can now consider mouth-feel, character as expressed through subtle flavours from the base ingredients, or quality cues such as organic accreditation or a superior water source. For anyone seeking to upgrade their favourite cocktail, you can choose a vodka that is really well-made and defined by a focus on quality, and that's a good development.

Finally, sum up Eight Lands in just three words.
Delicious. Organic. Unforgettable.

10

ESSENTIAL VODKAS TO TRY

Gone are the days when vodka's most appealing quality was its lack of flavour. Still, this spirit has always been at its best when purity is front and centre of the distiller's plans. There's never been a better time for vodkas which not only interpret this purity in their own way, but add a wonderfully dynamic flavour element, driven by the base ingredient of the spirit.

BEST IN GLASS «

» Connie Glaze
40% | Cornwall, UK
A craft gem from Tarquin Leadbetter's South Western Distillery (see page 196 for thoughts on his Cornish pastis). Connie Glaze is an homage to Cornwall's Constantine Bay, where the distillery is based, and this 100 per cent wheat-based distillate is filtered through purified sand to give it an extremely smooth mouthfeel. There's an ethical side too: one per cent of all the proceeds are donated to the Constantine Beach Guardians to keep it clean and unspoilt for years to come.

KEY

● WOODY		● SMOKY	
● NUTTY		● GREEN FRUIT	
● FLORAL		● RED FRUIT	
● MINERAL		● HERBAL	
● SWEETNESS		● SPICY	
● FATTY		● CITRUS	
● CEREAL		● VEGETAL	

» Broken Clock
40% | Cheshire, UK
The idea of 'lingering' seems out of step today. But for Broken Clock, it's fundamental. Inspired by the world's first astronomical clock and the subtle fruits of an English country garden, this is copper pot-distilled from wheat, then infused with a subtle home-grown apple element for a light, fruity aroma. One to take time over!

» Haku Vodka
40% | Kyushu, Japan
Suntory is best known for its revered whiskies (see page 122). However, it's also been making waves in the white spirit market since the 1950s. It recently created Haku: a rice wine-based spirit, which uses rice koji (a fermentation starter) and is pot-distilled then filtered through bamboo charcoal for a clean, floral note.

» Grey Goose Vodka
40% | Cognac, France
An icon. Since its 1997 introduction, Grey Goose has been *the* vodka which all other premium brands aspire to emulate. Distilled using single origin Picardie winter wheat and natural spring water from Cognac, Grey Goose is exceptionally clean as a spirit, with a slight touch of creaminess and a hint of soft cereal on the palate.

» Absolut Elyx
42.3% | Åhus, Sweden
Absolut is a worldwide megabrand but Elyx is something of an oddity. Created by master distiller Krister Asplund using a 1921 copper column still, Elyx is distilled from single-estate winter wheat grown in southern Sweden. The spirit is purified through copper 'packets' to remove sulphur compounds and ensure its smoothness.

» St George Green Chile
40% | California, USA
Creators of game-changing spirits since the early 1980s, St George has smashed it out of the park with Green Chile, a vodka infused with jalapeño, serrano, habanero and bell peppers, alongside lime juice and coriander. It has incredibly fresh, vegetal notes, alongside herbaceous and spice-laden heat. This will reinvent the Bloody Mary.

» Dima's Vodka
40% | Ukraine
A true story of strength in the face of adversity. When Russia invaded Ukraine, founder Dima Deinega's original production facility was closed due to extensive shelling, but now this organic, three-grain-based (barley, wheat and rye) spirit is once again thriving, and Dima's continues to give £1 a bottle to Ukrainian charities.

» Belvedere Heritage 176
40% | Żyrardów, Poland
One of the original premium vodkas, Belvedere has raised the game with its single estate bottlings, as well as Heritage 176, a rye-based spirit. Technically not a vodka, Heritage 176 is really an homage to the spirits of the past. It contains two per cent malt spirit, made from malting Dańkowskie rye by kiln toasting at 176°C (349°F). It is nutty and spicy with a toasted, sweet cereal note.

» Karlsson's Gold
40% | Gripsholm, Sweden
An absolute gem from Börje Karlsson, the master blender who developed the original recipe for Absolut in the 1970s. The secret behind this exceptional spirit is a blend of seven varieties of new potatoes, harvested before they have a chance to develop a firm skin. The spirit is distilled just once, to retain a smooth, sweet, creamy flavour and aroma.

» Blacklion
40% | Cotswolds, UK
Blacklion is the first European vodka made using sheep's milk, specifically from the Black Lion breed. The whey left over after cheese-making – which is surprisingly abundant in the necessary sugars to create a spirit – is fermented and triple-distilled. The result is noticeably smooth, creamy and silky on the palate.

OTHER
WORLD
SPIRITS

...which you need in your life

Within a mere handful of spirit categories, we've discovered countless unique flavour profiles, and some incredible history and culture too. However, outside this circle of familiar spirits lies an incredibly popular and relatively untapped area. The weird and wonderful drinks which may be vaguely familiar from trips abroad, but the DNA of which you'd be hard pushed to pinpoint. Each one of these drinks, of course, has a fabulous story to tell, and this chapter of the book will do just that.

ABSINTHE

The Mean, Green and (surprisingly) Versatile Machine

Earlier we lamented that, with its reputation as a drink to slam to get hammered, Tequila is one of the most misunderstood spirits in the world. But poor absinthe has perhaps suffered even more from some serious miscommunication issues. This vibrant, verdant and perfectly potent spirit has had quite the time of it, if you trawl back over its very chequered history of the last few hundred years. Frustratingly, absinthe continues to be one those spirits that very few drinkers venture towards, partly because of its notoriously high alcohol content – with some examples topping out at an eye-watering 70% ABV – and partly because of its bitter, herbaceous flavour. However, the main distraction comes from its supposedly hallucinogenic properties and the fact that a little over thirty years ago, absinthe was still on several countries' prohibited product lists.

Wormwood: The Heart of Absinthe

As gin is founded on juniper, so absinthe too is rooted in a single key botanical: *Artemisia absinthium*, or grand wormwood. This wild-growing herbaceous plant has been thought to contain medicinal properties since Ancient Egyptian times, and Ancient Greek physicians prescribed wormwood-infused wine (likely an unpalatable, bitter and dry concoction) for rheumatism and menstrual pain.

Despite its unpleasant taste, the theories on wormwood's properties persisted, and distilled tinctures were developed in the late 18th century. Pierre Ordinaire, a French doctor living in the Couvet area of Switzerland, created a cure-all tonic containing the herb. It proved popular and the recipe made its way into the hands of a commercial distiller, who began to make larger quantities of the spirit. As it gained popularity in Switzerland, its reputation spread across the French border – in particular to Pontarlier. The town which became the spiritual home of absinthe after Henry-Louis Pernod set up a distillery in 1805 to make this punchy herbaceous elixir.

The 1800s were a magical time for absinthe – especially in France. The spirit was very much at the heart of the *Belle*

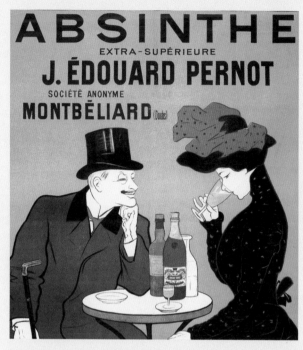

ABSINTHE
EXTRA-SUPÉRIEURE
J. ÉDOUARD PERNOT
SOCIÉTÉ ANONYME
MONTBÉLIARD (Doubs)

Époque: everyone from Vincent Van Gogh to Oscar Wilde seems to have been under its inspirational spell. Albert Maignan's *La Muse Verte* (1895) shows a poet succumbing to the effects of a 'Green Fairy', her hands clamped to his head as he swoons. Absinthe's reputation as a hallucinogenic comes from wormwood's supposedly psychoactive compound,

> ↑ *Absinthe was very much the drink-du-jour of the Belle Époque era in France.*

thujone – though there is no real scientific evidence to suggest thujone contains mind-altering powers at all.

By the 1900s, poor quality absinthe had spread through the market, often coloured with toxic chemicals such as copper arsenate. The spirit was a target for temperance advocates, who eventually got what they wanted: absinthe was banned first in Belgium in 1906, followed by the Netherlands; in its native Switzerland in 1910; in the USA two years later and finally – and fatefully – in France in 1915.

← *The impressively-shaped absinthe stills at the Combier distillery in the Loire Valley, France.*

PASTIS: ONE DOOR CLOSES...

With absinthe banished as a spirit-non-grata in 1915, distillers looked to fill the gap with something similar, but less offensive. By removing the wormwood, dialling up the anise, liquorice root and fennel notes and dialling down the ABV, French brands such as Pernod and Ricard were elevated to new heights. Domestic sales of both brands remain successful today.

HOW ABSINTHE IS MADE

Rather like gin, absinthe starts life as a conversation between a number of botanicals macerated in a neutral base spirit. This heady concoction, underpinned by wormwood, aniseed, fennel and other more aromatic herbs such as lemon balm, is then redistilled to a strength of around 72% ABV, where it can be bottled as a *blanche*, or clear absinthe. However, it can also be infused with other botanical essences post-distillation and coloured using natural chlorophyll or artificial green dyes to give it the vivid, vibrant hue most drinkers recognize. Absinthe is usually bottled at around 55–72% ABV, cementing its place in the canon of potent potables.

ENJOYING ABSINTHE

Much is made about its stupendously high strength but the most elegant way to unlock absinthe's flavours is to seek out a traditional 'French Method' absinthe fountain. Here iced water is slowly dripped into a glass upon which a decorative absinthe spoon holding a single cube of sugar has been placed. It's a mesmerizing sight to watch: as the sugar slowly dissolves into the drink the absinthe turns opaque, or *louche*, thanks to the insoluble oils in the spirit. Once this ritual is finished, you have a wonderfully complex drink, perfectly diluted and sweetened.

Joel & Neil's Perfect Serve

SAZERAC

Ok, so this isn't strictly an absinthe cocktail, as the primary spirits are Cognac and American rye whiskey. But the importance of the spirit in this highly flavoured drink cannot be underestimated. Absinthe participates here as a 'wash' – meaning that you rinse the glass out with a small amount to impart its aromatic goodness, without allowing its flavour to dominate. Be sure to put your serving glass in the freezer first.

HOW TO MAKE

* **ONE SUGAR CUBE**
* **ONE DASH PEYCHAUD'S BITTERS**
* **ONE PART COGNAC**
* **ONE PART RYE WHISKEY OR BOURBON**
* **TWO DASHES ABSINTHE**
* **LEMON PEEL, TO GARNISH**

Add the sugar cube and the bitters to a mixing glass, along with a small amount of the Cognac. Stir until dissolved. Add ice, the whisky and the rest of the Cognac and slowly stir for 15–20 seconds. Next, take your well-chilled serving glass from the freezer and add a couple of dashes of absinthe to it, making sure to run the liquid all the way around the inside of the glass to the brim. Pour out the excess then pour in the cocktail from the mixing glass and garnish with a small piece of fresh lemon peel.

MEET THE MAKER

} *Tarquin Leadbetter*

FOUNDER, SOUTHWESTERN DISTILLERY

You make a variety of pastis in Cornwall. Can you give us some details of how it is made and why it is unique?
We make our pastis like we make our gin: we gently steep botanicals overnight in wheat spirit before warming to distilling temperature in the morning. During eight hours or so of careful monitoring and adjusting, we collect only the heart of the run, discarding the first and last portions of the spirit. We then infuse more liquorice root and some fresh orange peel in the distillate. As far as we are aware it is the first brand of pastis to be created in the UK. There's more green aniseed than star anise, which adds lovely herbal notes and a delicious honey-like sweetness to the spirit.

What's the ethos behind your distillery?
Our ethos is simple: to make great-tasting spirits with integrity. What does this mean? To us, it is all about doing things properly. As far removed from mass-production as possible. We try to achieve this by going back to basics. Using traditional techniques, quality ingredients and old-fashioned equipment, staying true to our vision. Our copper pot still is fired by flame and judged by eye. We select our botanicals by sight and feel. And all our bottles are individually filled, corked, labelled, waxed and signed by hand.

What lessons have you learnt as a craft distiller?
Like many professions, I see distilling as something that you practice. And in such a way, it is something where your knowledge is continually expanding – we are always learning the craft. I designed the distillery myself and planned everything meticulously over two years, from the age of 23. But when put into practice, inevitably I had to learn everything the hard way... most importantly I would say I've learned to have a better sense of humour!

As a craft distiller, what keeps your passion ticking over?
There are those special moments in the day which remind you that you have the best job in the world: smelling fresh spirit come off the still, feeling that sensory rush of emotion; standing in front of 250 finished bottles ready to be boxed; experimenting with the new, weird and wonderful. Having started out my career working behind a desk for a big company, to me, there is nothing better than being your own boss. Blasting out loud music in the distillery, projecting films on the wall. Or being able to take the morning off work to go surfing!

Describe Southwestern Distillery in three words.
Spirits of integrity.

ARAK, OUZO & RAKI

Absinthe's Distant Cousins

From France to Lebanon, where you'll not only discover a phenomenal history of wine making (the Ancient Phoenicians were largely responsible for introducing vinification to Europe 2,500 years ago) but also of characterful spirit. Arak is the not-too-distant cousin to pastis and absinthe, sharing a similar heady, aromatic, aniseed-based flavour profile. Lebanese arak is made from the grapes of the last harvests in late September, which are then left to ferment in barrels for several weeks. The fermented grapes are distilled twice before aniseed is added.

In Greece, you'll encounter ouzo which, along with mastiha, is taken very seriously indeed. Historically the spirit was made in the same way as arak, using a grape-based distillate, to which aniseed would be macerated and redistilled. Today, ouzo is protected under EU law and its base spirit can come from other origins including molasses and different grain types. The very best examples of ouzo are those where the flavour has been 100 per cent derived from distilled botanicals, rather than the addition of post-distillation essences. However, when it comes to those aniseed flavours, distillers can explore a range of similar anethole-rich botanicals (the chemical flavour compound found in star anise, fennel and liquorice root) as well as flavours like cinnamon, clove and cardamom. When brought down to bottling strength (a minimum of 37.5% ABV) ouzo, like absinthe, *louches*

↑ Lebanese arak maturing in ceramic flagons (vessels).

nicely with the addition of water, where the full spectrum of flavours can be fully appreciated.

A highly honourable mention must go to Greece's other national spirit: mastiha. Mastiha (or mastika) is another pungent spirit (and also a lower ABV liqueur). The flavour is derived from the resin of the ancient mastic tree, which is macerated or distilled with spirit to produce a pine-led, savoury, herbal aroma.

Rather like arak and ouzo, raki is another spirit based around the hugely flavoursome properties of aniseed. Hailing from Turkey, where it has rightly become the national drink, raki takes its name from the Turkish and Arabic words for 'distilled'. It is made using the pomace of wine production, which is distilled into a very high strength spirit known as souma, first running from the stills at no higher than 94.5% ABV. Once the spirit is collected, it is then mixed with an aniseed flavourant – and sometimes another neutral, rectified high strength spirit – and distilled a second time, to a lower ABV (around 80%). It is then sweetened slightly and diluted down to bottling strength, before being rested in tanks for no fewer than 30 days, which allows the flavours to become more harmonized.

Like its other Mediterranean cousins, raki *louches* when mixed with water, bringing the intense herbal and spicy flavours to the fore, making it a great accompaniment with mezze dishes, fresh seafood and melon, the latter of which makes for a wonderfully refreshing pairing.

AKVAVIT

The true taste of the Nordics

A kvavit, or aquavit, is distilled from either grain (wheat or rye) or potatoes, and is emphatically Scandinavian in flavour. It emerged in the 1530s when, like many herbal spirits, *aqua vitae* – or the 'water of life' – was perceived to have medicinal properties. Then, in the 1700s, botanist Christopher Blix Hammer guided the spirit, writing extensively on how to utilize locally grown flavours for farm-distilled akvavit.

Each recipe is a closely guarded secret but, like absinthe and gin, must contain at its heart a specific single botanical, in this case caraway seed. It's often paired with a balanced spectrum of other herbs and spices, including cardamom, cumin, star anise, coriander, fennel and dill. It is distilled much in the same way as gin, with botanicals steeped in the base spirit before being distilled in a copper pot still or, more widely, on continuous column stills (see page 13). Some post-distillation flavouring is also allowed to heighten the intensity of the herbal flavours.

Frequently seen as a clear unaged spirit, akvavit can also be matured in oak casks, particularly ex-Sherry casks, to impart a richer note. Some are even 'sea aged' in casks stored on the deck of a boat taken down to the Equator and back – the motion of the ocean said to bring a more rounded character.

ENJOYING AKVAVIT

Scandinavian tradition dictates that akvavit is drunk chilled – or frozen – as a shot, often alongside a local beer, a variety of meats and cheeses and a hearty toast of *Skål!* (good health!) Historically, drinking in this way was thought to reduce the risk of food poisoning from poor quality meat, with the spirit killing off any nasty bugs. Today it is enjoying a renaissance with some of the best bartenders in the world using it in mixed drinks such as the Martini as well as in a Bloody Mary for a wonderful herbal twist.

SOJU

The Biggest Spirit in the World!

Yep, that's correct. Although you might never have heard of it, Korea's soju takes the top spot as the world's most successful spirit by volume. It's an accolade which Jinro, the brand of soju in question, has held for the past 20 years, consistently outselling the likes of Johnnie Walker blended Scotch, Bacardi rum and Stolichnaya vodka. In 2022 alone, Jinro sold a staggering 908 million litres of the stuff.

But what exactly is it? This clear rice wine-based distillate can trace its roots back to the 13th century, when the Mongols introduced distillation to the Korean Peninsula. It proved immensely popular and it has been estimated that by the early 20th century, there were in excess of 3,000 soju distilleries dotted across the region. The starch-heavy rice mash starts life as a solid mass, a kind of cake called a *nuruk*. This is essentially a fermentation starter to which yeast is added before it's mixed with water and cooked rice and fermented for up to 15 days.

Traditionally, soju was distilled in ceramic stills; today the more modern column method is typically employed before the spirit is diluted to bottling strength of between 12% and 25% ABV, with occasional post-distillation flavours and sweetness added in the form of apple and other fruits. This might seem low strength for a spirit, but that's really the point. It is enjoyed as part of a hugely popular shot culture, especially in Seoul and now more widely in the US, where the lower strength slips under the radar of the more highly taxed spirits.

ENJOYING SOJU

Most soju produced today is colourless and unaged, with rice as the primary ingredient. In the past, cheaper alternatives have been used, including potatoes and tapioca, when the Korean population faced a national shortage of rice. There's little by way of specific flavour in soju, but that means it lends itself perfectly to a beer pairing, with some consumers supercharging their brew by dropping in shots of soju. Its fresh, slightly sweetened-but-clean profile is also a great complement to dumplings, kimchi and sushi.

BAIJIU

The Savoury Spirit of China

While other western spirits such as Cognac and Scotch have found favour in mainland China, the same couldn't be said in reverse – until now. Baijiu, the savoury, characterful and enduring spirit produced domestically, possesses a unique flavour profile which is now gaining greater attention in the west.

THE FLAVOURS OF BAIJIU

There are four classifications of baijiu and around a dozen sub-categories, which makes it almost endlessly fascinating to connoisseurs and enthusiasts. *Nongxiang* or 'strong' style is bolder and spicier, with overripe tropical fruit, cocoa and wet hay notes (sometimes called a farmyard aroma). *Qingxiang* or 'light' style has more mellow fruits like watermelon along with more fragrant, herbal notes. *Jiangxiang* or 'sauce' style is yeasty, with bold fermented notes and earthy, dry, fragrant mushroom-like aromas. Finally, *mixiang*, or 'rice' style is floral and grassy, with notes of jasmine tea.

ENJOYING BAIJIU

C hina has been distilling baijiu for over 600 years, using dried, fermented sorghum grains as its base. The different baijiu-producing regions of China have their own specialized methods: in Sichuan, for instance, the fermented grains are left for up to a month in stone vessels, or in some locations they are buried in special pits to ferment. Once fermented, the relatively dry mash is distilled in vessels which allow steam to permeate and the alcoholic vapour is condensed into a pungent white spirit. It is aged in clay vessels porous enough to allow the spirit to mellow over time, typically for up to five years (and beyond in some exceptional cases). A blending process then takes place before the spirit is bottled – usually somewhere between a mild 38% ABV and a seriously punchy 65% ABV.

Domestically, it is mostly consumed as a room temperature shot: the *ganbei* or 'dry cup' style. To the untrained palate, baijiu can be an acquired taste – it's like trying a smoky Islay whisky for the first time. The more styles you try, the more the spirit begins to make sense and the complexities start to develop. A few bartenders are now starting to explore baijiu cocktails: it works surprisingly well in Mule-style drinks, or mixed with tonic and a little sweet vermouth.

SHOCHU

Big in Japan

ENJOYING SHOCHU

It depends on the style of shochu. The higher end *honkaku* styles tend to be enjoyed neat or with ice in a tumbler, or diluted with chilled or warm water, the latter really opening up the flavours of the base ingredients and adding to the mystery and complexity of the spirit. *Kōrui* styles are becoming more popular in mixed drinks and cocktails, with its neutrality making it incredibly versatile.

T he explosion of Japanese whisky has not only shaken up the global spirits market but had a huge impact on domestic spirits production too, with a greater appreciation for the country's distilling heritage. Hot on the heels of Japanese whisky comes shochu: a spirit distilled from barley, rice, buckwheat or potatoes, which have been fermented first with koji, a specific type of mould, bringing an umami note to the spirit. Mostly bottled unaged, shochu can be single distilled in what's called the *honkaku* style, which gives a more pronounced impression of its base ingredient and comes in at under 36% ABV. It can also be distilled multiple times in a column still (the *kōrui* style) and bottled at or below 45% ABV, which gives a more neutral, less characterful style of spirit. Shochu – and its close relation, awamori, a rice-based spirit native to the Okinawa prefecture of Japan – has broad flavour profiles, ranging from sweet dried flowers to coastal and saline or fermented orchard fruit notes. While mostly unaged, there is a growing trend for maturing more premium single distilled styles in cask to give even greater levels of complexity, with the results increasingly comparable to single malt whisky.

↖ Shochu is still the national spirit of Japan, despite the country's huge success with whisky production.

← The koji rice fermentation process used to make sochu.

10

ESSENTIAL WORLD SPIRITS *TO TRY*

With such incredible diversity, personality and production heritage, picking just ten world spirits to try is a fiendish task. But try we must! We hope this handful of our personal favourites will inspire you to go off on your own personal world spirit odyssey.

BEST IN GLASS «

» **Bareksten Aquavit**
40% | Blomsterdalen, Norway
Akvavit's spicy, caraway seed heart is truly the taste of Scandinavia. This version from award-winning Norwegian craft distiller Stig Bareksten has been created using a base spirit distilled from potatoes, caraway and a secret blend of other botanicals, before maturation in Oloroso Sherry casks. Big, bold spice and a smooth nutty character make this utterly unmissable.

KEY

- WOODY
- NUTTY
- FLORAL
- MINERAL
- SWEETNESS
- FATTY
- CEREAL
- SMOKY
- GREEN FRUIT
- RED FRUIT
- HERBAL
- SPICY
- CITRUS
- VEGETAL

» Ming River Sichuan Baijiu
45% | Sichuan, China
Beside Islay's smoky single malts, baijiu might just be one of the most acquired tastes in the spirits world, with its idiosyncratic savoury, malty, fermented flavour. Ming River has developed a more western style flavour profile, with fresh orchard fruits, a little peppery spice, pineapple and some coastal saltiness. Perfect in a Mule.

» 3S Mizunara Fut 1569 Conquête 2009 Shochu
41% | Kyushu, Japan
This cask-aged shochu, distilled at the Ohishi distillery back in 2009, is a revelation: the Mizunara cask (see page 18) has imparted a wonderful sandalwood aroma, with dark chocolate flavours on the palate. A great bridge between the world of single malt whisky and shochu.

» Tempus Fugit Vieux Pontarlier Absinthe
65% | Pontarlier, France
A wonderful absinthe, distilled using a Chardonnay grape-based spirit, with locally-sourced wormwood. It is a vibrant jade, with meaty, biscuity, almost saline notes alongside the anise. Perfectly balanced, with white pepper, mint and menthol rounding out the flavours.

» Tarquin's Cornish Pastis
42% | Cornwall, England
A genius play on words, and a wonderful play on the French classic too. Distiller Tarquin Leadbetter forages gorse flowers (which give a sweet coconut note) from the local cliff tops, distilling them with more traditional herbaceous botanicals, including anise and fresh orange peel.

» Tekirdag Rakisi No.10 Raki
47.5% | Turkey
Produced by Mey, the distillery behind the legendary Yeni Raki brand, Tekirdag is triple distilled in copper alembic stills from fresh grape spirit. It has a high anise content creating an intense *louche* when water is added, thanks to the abundance of flavoursome oils. Surprisingly silky, with a broad spiciness and direct herbal kick.

» El Massaya Arak
53% | Bekaa Valley, Lebanon
A traditional arak from one of Lebanon's leading distillers. This Obeidi grape spirit is distilled on a vine wood-fired still and flavoured using organic aniseed, then matured for two years in ceramic amphora vessels. It is bottled unfiltered, giving a wonderfully rounded, almost minty, herbal note with a long finish.

» Axia Extra Dry Mastiha
40% | Chios, Greece
Axia is a relatively new brand of mastiha but is already making huge waves in a previously niche category that is rapidly gaining global momentum. The resinous, almost pine-led notes are very prominent, before an earthy and very dry undertone, which lends itself well to more herbal or savoury cocktails. Try it in place of vodka in a Bloody Mary to make a Bloody Medusa, and you'll never look back.

» Wihayo Soju
19% | Schiedam, the Netherlands (!)
OK, a real curveball here. While soju is categorically Korean, we felt compelled to flag up this superb one. Wihayo Soju is made by lauded distiller Herman Jansen and Korean-Dutch food writer Nathalie Ji-Yun Kranenburg. It's made in the Korean way, using fermented rice and barley. Think fresh green apple, liquorice, a touch of maltiness, dried flowers and heather honey.

» Ryukyu 1429 Tsuchi Awamori
43% | Okinawa, Japan
Awamori is a shochu-style spirit which can only be produced on the Japanese island. Ryukyu distil several styles: an unaged *mizu* (water), a five year aged *kaze* (air) and this one, *tsuchi* (earth), aged in traditional clay pots. Marzipan and mineral notes, ripe orchard fruit aromas, and an earthy, leafy, mushroom-led flavour, with cocoa powder and a dusting of white pepper. Unusual, but delightful.

NO-LO

a remarkable oxymoron of flavour!

The impact of no and low-alcohol offerings on both the culture of socialising and the wellbeing of drinkers is extraordinary. In 2022, the market value of this category reached $11 billion globally – and is forecast to grow another third by 2026, according to the Institute of Wine and Spirit Research (IWSR). This not only demonstrates that drinkers are happy to make a more temperate choice but also that the whole industry is willing to embrace new brands and experiment with non-alcoholic cocktails and serves that don't feel in any way inferior to their traditional versions.

So why the huge surge in growth? Over the past five years, the quality of these 'No-Lo spirits' (can something that doesn't contain alcohol actually be called a spirit..?) has undoubtedly improved. However, more importantly, so has the vision of the people developing them. No longer are new companies looking to simply emulate existing spirit categories; instead, creative thinkers are looking at popular serves, food pairings and – most importantly – the simple matter of great taste.

SO JUST HOW ARE
NO-LO SPIRITS MADE?

For years, creating a credible –
and tasty – spirit without the alcohol content
seemed nigh on impossible. The inherent complexity of
a spirit is intensified by the distillation process, so those
attempting to develop non-alcoholic version had to
resort to other means – without much success.

However, there have been intriguing scientific developments in the removal of the actual alcohol from a beverage. Some no-lo drinks are initially distilled from a beer or wine like a regular spirit. The alcohol molecules are then removed post-distillation by a third re-distillation stage that separates the hydrophobic alcohol molecules from the water and flavour molecules. This allows the 'spirit' to keep most of the characteristics of the original, including the distinctive mouthfeel – though as a result, a number of these styles of spirit have a residual level of alcohol left. In the UK, this cannot measure more than 0.5% ABV.

Another option is to use what is called a hydrosol – this involves distilling water or tea and adding specific flavourings – such as ginger and citrus elements, salts, acids and flavour stabilisers – to mimic the flavour and mouthfeel of a spirit. This can also be combined with other flavourings such as gin botanicals and spices and, in the case of low-ABV spirits, a small amount of spirit such as gin. This results in a concentrated, realistic spirit flavour. Adding a little glycerol post-distillation can also help bring the 'unctuousness' of an alcoholic spirit.

Other producers simply pack their recipe with a greater intensity of extracts or botanicals, using infusion to bring through the characterful flavours. What they lack in authenticity, they make up for in flavoursome punch.

Styles Of No-Lo Spirits

Botanical spirits – those which most emulate gin and other herbal-based spirits – have so far dominated the category. The market leader is Seedlip, a brand launched by drinks entrepreneur Ben Branson in 2015. Now there are also a number of superbly made botanical spirits that aren't aiming to directly replace spirits but go their own way. Three Spirit, for example, makes drinks with mood-enhancing ingredients to complement a specific time, place or moment – the Livener (see page 216), or the Nightcap, for example. There are also a number of 'aged spirit' non-alcoholic equivalents, such as spiced rum and whisky. This is a much more difficult style to master given the dynamic twists and complexity maturation brings to a spirit.

↓ *A retail store dedicated to Lo-No products, such as the Club Soda Tasting Room & Shop in London, is becoming a serious reality in today's fast growing marketplace.*

MAKING YOUR OWN
Non-Alcoholic Cocktail

RASPBERRY SHRUB

There are a number of credible 'no-lo' alternatives to use in place of your usual gin or rum when making a cocktail. But you don't need to shell out on another bottle if you fancy something delicious, complex and alcohol-free. The shrub cocktail (using fruit-based vinegar) has long been favoured by bartenders looking for tart, direct flavours, with the acidity helping to really capture the palate. When balanced correctly, vinegar gives a crisp, spirit-like feel to a cocktail, which works exceptionally well when paired with fresh fruit purée, herbs and bitters.

HOW TO MAKE

TONIC
WATER

BALSAMIC VINEGAR

LIME JUICE

RASPBERRY
PURÉE

* **TWO PARTS FRESH RASPBERRY PURÉE OR A REGULAR FRUIT SMOOTHIE**

* **HALF PART FRESH LIME JUICE**

* **QUARTER PART BALSAMIC VINEGAR**

* **THREE DASHES OF CHOCOLATE OR BLACK WALNUT BITTERS**

* **FOUR PARTS TONIC WATER**

* **FRESH BASIL LEAF, TO GARNISH**

Add all the ingredients except the tonic water to a shaker. Half fill with ice and shake for 5–8 seconds. Strain into a Champagne flute, add a couple of ice cubes and top with tonic water, stirring gently. Garnish with a fresh basil leaf. Try the same recipe using fresh strawberry purée for a slightly more fragrant, sweeter drink.

MEET
THE
MAKERS

Abbey Ferguson,
Lexie Lancaster &
Lauren Chitwood

FOUNDERS, SPIRITLESS

Tell us a little bit about yourself and the concept of Spiritless.
Spiritless was founded by three women in Louisville, Kentucky. We were working together producing events for some of the biggest spirits brands in the world; all the while, we were busy mothers, and we felt the grind of alcohol. Although we weren't necessarily looking to be totally sober, we wanted a tool to be able to enjoy and participate without regret. The three of us built a makeshift still and started tinkering with removing the alcohol of full proof bourbon off the shelf. Today, we have a patented process that allows us to make the best tasting non-alcoholic spirits in the world.

What's the biggest challenge you face on a day-to-day basis?
Being a founder requires constant prioritisation. There are endless opportunities and priorities when you are scaling a business; using time wisely and effectively for the greatest impact for the company is both the most challenging but most important part of the job.

What's the secret behind creating a great non-alcoholic brand and what do you look for in every Spiritless release?
Spiritless has established a reputation to uphold – we make incredible and surprisingly authentic tasting non-alcoholic spirits. We don't bring anything to market if we don't love the liquid in the glass.

How do you drink it at home?
It depends on the day. During the week, we love a ginger non-alcoholic Margarita with Spiritless Jalisco 55 and our Horse's Kick ginger syrup. On the weekends, we're probably making a Halfsies Old Fashioned with both our Kentucky 74 (see page 217) and a favourite local Kentucky bourbon.

Finally, sum up Spiritless in just three words.
Less. Is. Yes!

10
ESSENTIAL
NO-LO
SPIRITS
TO TRY

Decided to take things a little easier in the alcohol department? There's never been a better time for a spirit lover to dial down their consumption: whether you want to replicate the flavour of your favourite tipples, or bring a fresh perspective to the night ahead.

BEST
IN
GLASS
«

» Three Spirit Livener
0% | London UK
Three friends with backgrounds that cover plant science, distilling and the bar world are behind Three Spirit, whose mantra is providing 'functional spirit alternatives'. The Livener delivers by blending herb, distillates and ferments with adaptogens and nootropics – ingredients with alleged mood-boosting or cognitive-enhancing properties – including Lion's Mane mushrooms, Schisandra berries, guayusa, hops and cacao. Livener is full of vibrant berries and warming, zesty notes.

KEY

WOODY	SMOKY
NUTTY	GREEN FRUIT
FLORAL	RED FRUIT
MINERAL	HERBAL
SWEETNESS	SPICY
FATTY	CITRUS
CEREAL	VEGETAL

» Portobello Road Temperance
4.2% | London, UK
One of the best, most fully flavoursome low ABV gins we've discovered. Jake Burger, of the Portobello Road distillery, focused on what he does best: creating world-class gin, but low ABV. Temperance delivers the botanical punch of a London Dry with a softer, citrus spice and stands up well in any classic gin cocktail.

» Wilderton Earthen
0% | Oregon, USA
Over several years, drinks industry veterans Brad Whiting and Seth O'Malley utilized their distilling expertise and extensive botanical library to create a range of different expressions. Earthen is a spicy, exotic-tasting dark spirit alternative which brings white peppercorn, pine-smoked tea and cardamom as the main flavours.

» Wavelength Amber Digestif
0% | Cornwall, UK
Wavelength (formerly Highpoint) has taken the aperitif market head on with its inspired creations. Amber Digestif's base ferment is infused for 30 days with a range of botanicals and spices including lapsang, ginger, clove and cacao nibs, and a wonderfully bittersweet note of vanilla, bonfire toffee, smoke and dry oakiness.

» Lyre's Agave Blanco Spirit
0% | London, UK
From rum to gin, bourbon to Tequila, Lyre's has sought non-alcoholic solutions in existing drinks categories and developed highly credible versions that work especially well in classic cocktails. This agave-style spirit comes very close to the herbal, citrus taste of a great *blanco* Tequila and is really nice in a Margarita or Paloma.

» Spiritless Kentucky 74
0% | Kentucky, USA
Kentucky 74 succeeds in emulating the flavours of bourbon and proved many doubters wrong by delivering sweet, vanilla-led oakiness and soft cherry and tobacco notes, backed up by a touch of smoke. The acid test was whether it made a good Old Fashioned. The answer? A resounding yes.

» Seedlip Grove 42
0% | Beaconsfield, UK
It would be churlish not to include the pioneers of the no-lo movement here. Seedlip, the world's first distilled non-alcoholic spirit, has had a remarkable decade of growth since the brand was set up in 2015. With its three expressions (the herbal Garden 108, citrus-led Grove 42 and aromatic Spice 94), Seedlip is still pushing boundaries.

» GABA Sentia Red
0% UK
A very unusual alcohol-free spirit indeed, Sentia was developed by Professor David Nutt, who researches how the brain reacts to gamma-aminobutyric acid, a chemical that heightens relaxation. Sentia aims to give that 'two drink feeling' without the side effects of alcohol. Fruity, with a dark, bitter herbal spiced note, it has a touch of vermouth or Campari about it.

» Atopia Spiced Citrus
0.5% | Dufftown, Scotland
Atopia was developed by Lesley Gracie, master distiller at Hendrick's Gin, in an attempt to bring the specific flavours of gin successfully into the No-Lo category. Spiced Citrus is the most successful of the trio of expressions on offer, combining distillates of orange, juniper, coriander, angelica root and lemon rather well indeed.

» Almave Ámbar
0% | Jalisco, Mexico
A noteworthy celebrity collaboration. Almave was founded by Formula One legend Lewis Hamilton and agave spirits expert, Iván Saldaña Oyarzábal. It is the first non-alcoholic spirit to be produced in the same way as Tequila, using Weber Blue agave but without fermentation. The taste is authentic, warming and herbaceous, sharing a great deal with a cask-aged *reposado* Tequila.

Index

Cocktails are in *italics*

Acknowledgements

Thanks to the following folks for all their help and support in making *In Fine Spirits* come to life:

Alison Starling, Jeannie Stanley, Jonathan Christie, Pauline Bache and the incredible team at Octopus, our wonderful agent Martine Carter at Sauce Management, Andrew Montgomery for his peerless photography, Richard Bates, Nikki Burgess, Emily Harris, DK Cheung, Beccy Smith, Matt Sykes, Carlotta Colkin, Barney Wilczak, Desmond Payne, Trudiann Branker, Farah Yaqub, David Rodriguez, Eduardo Gomez, Lucy Francis, Rob Samuels, Lily Wiggins, Charlotte Pederson, Kirsty Black, Patrice Piveteau, Kate Sweet, Catalina Bentz, Francois Thibaut, Olivia Butcher, Tarquin Leadbetter, Lauren Chitwood, Jake Burger, Chris Papple, Alex Christou and the team at Channel 4's *Sunday Brunch*.

PICTURE CREDITS

Special photography Andrew Montgomery for Octopus Publishing Group

Octopus Publishing Group would like to acknowledge and thank the following for providing images for this book.

Akg-images Universal Images Group/Universal History Archive 29; Fototeca Gilardi 179a; **Alamy Stock Photo** World History Archive 13; Horst Friedrichs 15a; Fraser Band 16; Associated Press 19; Universal Images Group North America LLC 31; Bill Waterson 33; Album 37; Chronicle 51; blickwinkel 54; Chris Hellier 55b; Art Collection 70; imageBROKER 73; Image Professionals 92; Horst Friedrichs 104; Shawshots 106; Granger Historical Picture Archive 108; Trinity Mirror/Mirrorpix 109a; Pictorial Press 113a; Jekaterina Sahmanova 129b; Olivier Roux/ SagaPhoto 132; Cephas Picture Library 141; Chronicle 142; Robert Harding 143; Andrew Lloyd 157;

MBP-one 159r; Mauritius Images 165a; Heritage Image Partnership 178; The Print Collector 179b; Associated Press 192l; Panther Media 198; CPA Media Pte Ltd 205l; John Lander 205r;

Dreamstime Dplett 17; Panama00 30; Maximfesenko 57; Fotoviejo 76a; Richard Ellis 76b; Drserg 103; Skopal 164; Bhofack2 188; Cegli 193; David68967 200; Keechuan 201; Limyongheng 203; **Getty Images** Bloomberg 34; Alfredo Martinez 72; Pedro Pardo 82; Keystone-France 109b; swim ink 2 137; Georges Gobet 138; Geography Photos 155; Houston Chronicle/ Hearst Newspapers 163; Cris Bouroncle 165b; Jonathan Knowles 172; Jonathan Nackstrand 180; Matt Cardy 181l; NurPhoto 204; **iStock** ArtistGNDphotography 18; 24 5PH; GummyBone 55a; camaralenta 75a, 83a; Jose de Jesus Churion 75b; Heiko119 96; stevanovicigor 97; images-twiston 98; GAPS 129a; viennetta 145; Tanya145 181r; Jonathan Wilson 202; andresr 208; Maryna

Voronova 211r; **Pexels** Karolina Grabowska 38; **Shutterstock** barmalini 36; Victor Moussa 53r; aindigo 81; Kelly vanDellen 100b; Ralf Liebhold 102; Everett Collection 107a; Sergiy Palamarchuk 107b; LightField Studios 124; barmalini 130a & b; Anna Kepa 150; **SuperStock** Aurélien Brusini/hemis.fr; **TopFoto** Interfoto 12; Fine Art Images/Heritage Images 191;

Unsplash Edward Howell 66; Stephan Hinni 71; Joel de Vriend 100a; Gabriella Clare Marino 177.

Thanks to the following for additional imagery.

Courtesy Bacardi: 52r, photo Manny Rodriguez 87; Beam Suntory 110; Bushmills 113b; Chichibu 111a; Club Soda 211l; Durham Distillery, North Carolina 15b; Etter Distillerie 158a & b, 159c; Irish Distillers Ltd 112; Kanosuke 111b; Laird & Company 162l & r; Lustau 154; Pernod Ricard 43, 44; Vinprom-Troyan 159l